John Widdup

**The doom of Mac Diarmid**

An oriental legend of the Gael

John Widdup

**The doom of Mac Diarmid**
*An oriental legend of the Gael*

ISBN/EAN: 9783337150945

Printed in Europe, USA, Canada, Australia, Japan

Cover: Foto ©ninafisch / pixelio.de

More available books at **www.hansebooks.com**

# THE DOOM OF MAC DIARMID;

## An Oriental Legend of the Gael.

BY

JOHN WIDDUP, A.B., T.C.D., L.R.C.S.I.

Author of an Essay on Physical Astronomy.

DUBLIN:
R. D. WEBB & SON, PRINTERS, 74, ABBEY STREET.
1874

To His Excellency the Duke of Abercorn,

LORD LIEUTENANT GENERAL AND GENERAL GOVERNOR OF IRELAND,

THE FOLLOWING LEGEND, BY HIS GRACIOUS PERMISSION,

IS RESPECTFULLY DEDICATED

BY HIS OBEDIENT SERVANT,

THE AUTHOR.

# PREFACE.

In the reign of Shah Hussein, who has been described as one of the most bigoted sovereigns that ever ruled over Persia, although of an indolent and rather mild disposition, the various provinces of that country experienced greater miseries than under the most cruel depotism.

Mirvais, an Afghan nobleman, who had resided for some time at the court of Isfahan, determined to render his native land independent, and for this purpose invited the principal Persian governors thereof to a banquet at Candahar; where in the midst of the revels they were assassinated by a number of youths disguised in female apparel.

The facility whereby Mirvais subsequently dispersed the royal troops from Afghanistan, and became chief of that province, induced him to raise his ambitious views even to the throne of Persia. He was however prevented by death from accomplishing his design.

Mir Maghmud, his son and successor, of equal ambition, though of inferior talent, intent on the same scheme, collected a large number of the discontented inhabitants throughout the kingdom, particularly tribes of Tartars and natives of the Kerman mountains—friends of his father—and with these combined forces marched at once towards Isfahan.

In the vicinity of the city he was met by the king's army hastily assembled, over which he gained a signal and unexpected victory—he himself being about to take flight previous to the conclusion of the engagement.

The legend commences with a brief description of the battle. Gulnabad was situate in the immediate neighbourhood of Isfahan.

It cannot escape the reader's observation that the antient terms, particularly the proper names in the Persian language, which have been transmitted to us, bear so close a resemblance to the names indicating the same objects in the Irish vernacular, as to produce a confident belief that the language of both countries must have been once identical.

# THE DOOM OF MAC DIARMID,

## An Oriental Legend of the Gael.

### CANTO I.

GULNABAD, thy fields are bright,
   Yet 'tis not with the orient beam;
Yon sudden glow of crimson light
   Is not of Heaven's æthereal stream.
Yon dense and darkly moving cloud,
   Whose rolling columns float afar,
Is not the pure aerial shroud
   Was wont to greet the morning star.
Why bursts that dread tremendous sound
   Rending thy still and peaceful vale?
Why wave the hostile banners round
   The dawn-lit hill and lovely dale?
Sure frantic Discord might be sent
   To rule a less endeared domain,
Where rugged mountains ocean rent
   Repel the boisterous hurricane;
There storm-nursed on the billow's foam,
   While wind and wave contending rise,

Proud she'd enjoy her peaceless home
   Exulting as the daylight dies.
To turmoil doomed in scene so meet,
   Be Discord with her horrors sad,
Far from the groves and gardens sweet
   Of thy fair vale, dear Gulnabad.

The passing zephyr's gentle breath
Wafts off the lingering smoke of death.
The thunder for a moment still
No longer echoes from the hill;
While blushing from the East a flood
Of brightness robes the scene of blood.
O'er verdant plain and blooming bower,
That welcomed oft the morning hour,
Smiling in perfume, as to pay
Its sweetness to the new-born day,
Foul havoc and revenge arise
To desecrate a paradise.

The Persian, host on host arrayed,
In battle panoply displayed,
   Raise the loud shout to Allah's name.
Each rank exhorting, chiefs of fame,
Rostam, Abdallah, Merdan fly
With prayers to conquer or to die.
As undulating in the sheen
Flaunted his banner gold and green,
The noble Rostam raised his sword,
The good, the gallant Georgian lord.

## CANTO I.

"On, on to victory," he cried,
"Iberia's sons, Iberia's pride:
Before you cowers the deadly foe,
  Who fraudfully your sires betrayed.
Let the base blood of Mirvais flow,
  Till treason in the dust be laid.
Let Persia, from each province see
  Iberia rushing to the war.
Spare not one rebel Abdolee,
  Revenge the loss of Candahar."

While reining back his fiery steed,
  The Arab chief Abdallah heard,
The valiant Georgian forward speed,
  And grievously in heart deterred,
Lest Rostam might a conquest claim,
And cast a stigma on his name,
He orders forth the dense array
Of Arab's light-armed cavalry;
Who hail the summons with a cheer,
And brandish high the glittering spear.
Like gushing torrents they unite
With Georgia's powerful band their might;
Spear, scimitar, and axe, and targe
Clash as they thundered to the charge.

Then echoed hill and dale around,
Responsive to the awful sound;
As if the earth's broad base were riven,
And once again to chaos given.

Such boundless uproar wildly rose,
As fierce encountering columns close;
'Twould seem to start the mouldering dead
Where Rostam and Abdallah led.

The troops of Candahar survey'd
Impending ruin undismay'd.
Maghmud, their haughty prince, implored
Brave Ullah, Kerman's warlike lord,
To join with force increased the band,
He loved to govern and command.
He quickly of the central van,
Insurgents from Mazanderan,
A squadron led, then eastward turned,
To join his troop whom vengeance burned.

Firm and resolved the heroes stood,
From Kerman's land of hill and flood;
They little deemed whose power they swell,
If war upon their tyrants fell.
They recked not where destruction's dart
Might aim, so 'twould but reach the heart
Of him whose execrated sway
Had swept their altar's fire away.

" Great source of light, eternal fire !
Revered alike by son and sire,"
Ullah exclaimed, " though fate should doom
Our future to the silent tomb,

Within our hearts diffuse the flame
Our fathers felt for Iran's name ;
Who conquering an eternal fame,
Joy'd even in pangs of death to see
Her altar pure, her temple free."

Mir Maghmud saw, with proud delight,
Ullah condensing to the fight—
His vaward wing, prepared to meet
The threatening storm's impending weight.
He then despatched a mandate brief
That Oman, the bold Tartar chief,
Should let the cannons' roaring breath
Ply instantly the work of death ;
Then from the right with sword and spear,
Assail the Persian cannoneer.

As the cataracts raging roar,
When from the rocks their torrents pour.
As the deep surges heave below,
That boiling, meet them as they flow ;
So on the left of Maghmud's line
 The Georgian and the Arab fell,
Whom Kerman's spearmen, at a sign,
 Like granite rocks the waves, repel.

The sanguined stream o'erflows the field
Of victims slain, who scorned to yield.
No recreant thought of flight or fear,
Though bayonet, arquebus and spear

More surely weave the veil of death,
Than the sirocco's poisoning breath.
Hark! through the clamor of the fray
Great Rostam bursts his dreadful way.
Many a pale and quivering corse
Lay crushed beneath the Georgian horse,
On, on unchecked, uncurbed they ran,
The line they break, and through the van,
With hoof immersed in hostile gore
Dark death in crimsoned torrents pour.

As the red lightning cleaves the rock,
As the terrific earthquake's shock,
The harbingers of death now fly
From carronade and musketry.
Ere Merdan could the charge refrain
Of Persia's life guards, on the plain
A thousand pale and prostrate lay,
Struck from the hostile battery.
Yet still with ardor unallayed,
He urged each chief to join and aid
His severed wing with strength combined,
And each his separate charge assigned.
With these the stern desire arose
To rush amidst their Tartar foes—
With vengeance deep, with kindling ire
Their hearts are fraught, their souls are fire.

Such latent force, ere bursting loud,
Concentrates the electric cloud;

Though calm in its incipient birth,
And still and silent as the earth,
When shaded with the pall of night,
Ere morn unveils her brow of light;
Yet soon resounding, peal on peal
Its awe inspiring course reveal;
Descending from its orbit high,
Huge blackened masses prostrate lie
Of art and nature, tree and tower,
Blighted and rent proclaim its power.


Amazed was Maghmud to behold
Persians in armour chased with gold,
Reform their ranks, present a line
Unbroken, at their leader's sign.
The veterans of his army fly
   Eager to combat at his call,
And rushing with him fearlessly
   On Merdan and his column fall.
O'er the wide field, the deaf'ning sound
   Of their fell conflict thrilled the air;
Their shouts the very brave astound,
   And strike the timid with despair.


The Persian with redoubled rage
   The onset to repel aspires.
From Merdan's arm though stiff with age
   The bravest of the foe retires.

Yet still in multitudes untold,
    They come, projecting spear on spear,
In hopes of spoil, determined, bold,
    To grace in death a gory bier.

Wearied, faint, with wounds oppressed
    Merdan now combats ; at his side
The brave, the flower of Persia rest,
    Who prompt for king and country died.
Beset, his hauberk pierced and riven
    With Afghan spears, when to his aid,
There came, like Peri sent from heaven,
    A youth in Georgian garb arrayed ;
Who, fatal as the lava stream,
    Advanced to meet the rebel foe,
When from the mountain's towering flame,
    Its desolating torrents flow.
The hands that Merdan's bosom sought,
    Fall reeking to the blood stained dust ;
Maghmud, appalled, no longer fought,
    But cursed the prophet as unjust :
His veterans too avoid the fray,
    Achmed the Georgian marks their flight,
And as the eagle seeks his prey,
    He follows with avenging might.

Merdan is rescued ; but while late
    Young Achmed the pursuit detained,
Inscrutable ! astounding fate !
    Oman the royal battery gained.

And thence its booming thunders aimed
   On the astonished Persian host,
Who pause, no more with ardour flamed,
Exclaiming yet with souls untamed,
" Have arms from hell our battle crossed ?
Or treason dark our triumph lost ? "

The Arab first deserts the field,
All but the Georgian squadron yield.
Yet ere the chief Abdallah fled,
Rostam was numbered with the dead,
Who faintly uttered to his band,
" I perish by a traitor's hand."

No more was heard.  The desperate strife
His troop maintained, till ebbing life
Flowed in warm currents from each heart,
That scorned from its chief to part,
Though his last mortal pang was o'er,
His voice could now inspire no more.

\*    \*    \*    \*    \*

The turmoil of the battle's done,
   The victor's shouts now die away,
The toil is o'er, the triumph won,
   And ceased the carnage of the fray.
The mellowed sombre tints of eve
Around the scene their mantle weave,
Silence uninterrupted, deep
And solemn seems alone to weep

Above the dead, who blithely gave
Their life blood to bedew their grave.

\* \* \* \* \*

What lonely warrior lingers now?
Seen dimly by night's dusky brow
On yonder mound, where pallid lie
The embers of mortality.
The pensive, yet impressive air,
The mournful look of calm despair
Portray the flow of passions tide
His soul o'erwhelmed. He seemed to chide
The tardy moon, whose feeble light
No object yet revealed to sight.

Faltering tones arrest his ear,
That plaintive flow from sorrow near;
He paused to list; but all was still,
Save the light zephyr on the hill;
The watchword, he had heard that morn
Throughout the tents of Persia borne,
He uttered loud, when lo! there came
In sounds distinctly heard his name.
"Give aid, brave Achmed, Georgia's pride,
If thine the friendly voice I hear;
Behold where wounding breast and side,
Glanced the sharp point of Ullah's spear.
Reach from beside yon fallen steed,
The ample turban there you'll find;
Haste, lest I exhausted bleed,
'Tis round yon Arab's temple twined."

With speed advancing, Achmed found
The chieftain Herman prostrate thrown;
The turban o'er his wound he bound,
Where the rude weapon bared the bone.
His pain he soothed, and then with hope,
The veteran cheered, whom oft he knew
Exultingly with danger cope,
And in her direst haunts pursue.

Rapidly he sought a car,
To bear him from the field afar.
And straight conveyed him, lorn and sad,
To thy domed halls, sweet Gulnabad.

" Herman, I fondly deemed," he said,
" Where thou wert prostrate with the dead,
Our prince still living might be found
Extended on yon ghastly mound;
But profitless, alas! and vain,
It were to seek our chief again;
The gallant Rostam ne'er could bide
  A beam of heaven's own light,
That saw amidst the purple tide
Of Persia's battle, scattered wide,
  Her sons' dishonored flight."

"Too true," said Herman, " but his fate
To no opponent's arm was due,
The treacherous Arab's deadly hate
Our generous leader slew.

While charging the proud rebel's host,
The battle to retrieve ere lost,
Abdallah struck him with his spear
Through the left side—then pale with fear
The dastard viewed and quit the field;
But had I not been forced to yield
To fainting swoon, from loss of blood,
With this good poinard I'd have sped,
To meet the caitiff ere he fled,
And stab him where he stood."

Deep anguish clouded Achmed's brow
And thrilled each fibre of his heart.
" This deed of horror, Herman, now
We'll briefly to the king impart;
He will not spare the traitor's life,
Who in the tumult of the strife,
With his accursed hand,
By foulest murder has o'erthrown
The noblest pillar of the throne,
The guardian of his land.

" In sooth thou little knowest the court,
    By evil agents swayed,
Our gentle monarch is their sport,
    To Arab wiles betrayed.
Rostam, 'tis true, he dearly loved,
And chiefly by his counsel moved,
When from his mountain home our prince,
    Summoned, to court would come;

But now 'tis just to fear that since
   His melancholy doom
Abdallah will more power assume,
Whose deep dyed guilt, should we presume
With truth and courage to arraign,
Our utmost efforts would be vain.
Though pure the Christian, how his tale
Against an Emir would avail,
Who thrice sojourned at Mecca's shrine;
Whom priest and people deem divine,
Thou mayest surmise, I but foresee
From present grief more misery.

" Yet nought should thy desire retard
Our king against such foes to guard;
Haste to the court, the meidan gain,[1]
Let no ulterior duty bar
Thy speed to Hussein, though in vain,
You may plead at the Chilminar.[2]

# THE DOOM OF MAC DIARMID,

## An Oriental Legend of the Gael.

### CANTO II.

The dome and the spire are radiant with day,
    O'er Isfahan's people in prayer,
The grove and the terrace no longer are gay
    With the smile of the young and the fair.
The voice and the lyre of the minstrel are mute,
    No procession in triumph appears,
With melody heard from the sweet warbling lute,
    But there's war-wrought affliction and tears.

An alcove of the palace, raised
On pure white marble pillars, blazed
With gorgeous beauty. Mirrors threw
A thousand rays of crimson hue
With gold and purple tints combined,
From lattices with roses twined,
Which silken folds within adorn
To simulate the blush of morn.

Prone on a couch a maiden lay,
As seen by the rich dawn-like ray;
Her sable tresses unconfined
Bedecked the couch where she reclined;
A small white hand, beneath her head,
Scarce veiled the copious tears she shed;
The ottoman her arm upheld,
Whose snowy velvet nought excelled
In purity of tinge, the limb
Rounded and tapering; but how dim
All other objects loomed to sight,
When as her form she raised,
Her darkling eyes of heavenly light
Around in sadness gazed.

What roving zephyr rustling waves
The pepul boughs, the roses leaves?[1]
'Tis not the breeze, for in their shade,
Achmed approached and mournful said,
"Mindah, be comforted, the king
Alone omnipotent, can bring
Again the happiness that late
Our hopes enjoyed, ere Rostam's fate
Plunged into misery the land.
How gladly with his Georgian band,
He would have all from ruin saved,
Had not his life been foully reaved."

In mourning terms of sweetest tone
Mindah exclaimed, Oh! Heaven alone!

Rostam fallen! my guardian sire!
Oh! would that in the blazing pyre,
From which in childhood I was freed
By him who loved each noble deed,
And lived by saintly virtues blessed,
I destined were in peace to rest,
With those to whom existence owed
Its parentage; the awful load
Of misery that now impends
O'er princesses, bereft of friends,
Had ne'er been known; the silent tomb
Had saved me from an orphan's doom."

"Grieve not unhopingly, dear maid;
    One earthly guardian lost,
Kind heaven preserving to thine aid
    Of friends a countless host;
The veterans of our mountain horde,
    Inured to war's wild scene,
Will joyfully their lives afford
    To guard their favorite queen."

"Old Herman, dauntless chief, yet lives,
Whose wisdom sure protection gives;
Him you have seen so oft alone
Admire with awe thy diamond zone,
Raising mysteriously his eyes,
As if to inspiration given,
Regarding thee with mute surprise
As angel sent from heaven;

Whose mission the All-wise above,
In pity to the human race,
Conceded, and that like the dove,
You came a messenger of peace."


"No more, dear Achmed, let no dream
    Or vain delusion e'er inspire
Thy soul with fancies which may seem
    Meet to the aged.  Devouring fire,
Amid war's desolating strife,
    Consumed our native palace walls,
Each friend beloved, each parent's life
    Was doomed amidst their halls ;
When rescued from the burning pile,
    In infancy, no thought remained
To memory, save a mother's smile
Of placid love—endearing wile—
    That o'er my spirit blessings rained.


"This girdle, on whose front is traced
    The cross with signs which few can read,
From Herman's mind all thought effaced,
    Save one, the emblem of our creed.
To him imbued in Christian lore
    An orphan borne from distant lands,
With sign so blessed could ne'er adore
    In temples raised by pagan hands.
I know not how my thoughts unfold
    When lights upon our altar burn—

" Some wonted mystic rites of old
    That make my childhood's days return;
  Visions appear, as if yon sun²
    Stored sacred beams to light our fanes,
  And the celestial flame, thence won,
    Absolved in air all mortal stains.

" Lo! now, yon mosque, whose portals wide
  Pour forth the ever surging tide
  Of rushing fanatics—some ban
  Of Eblis sure or Ahriman,
  'Twould seem had made their souls recede
  From Christian rite, or holy deed;
  Or faith arrayed in sacred love
  Inspiring them to soar above
  Each mundane impulse—passion, hate—
  They madly deem the will of fate.

" Then why predict, that one whose path
    Is aye beset with mortal toil,
  Could mar war's desolating wrath,
    Or turn the victor from the spoil.

" Oh no! to flee remote from scenes
    Where death makes havoc of our friends,
  And courtesy all smiling feigns
    A friendship that misfortune ends;
  To Georgia's vales and Tiflis' towers,
    Where life's smooth current calmly played,
  Where bloom the ever grateful bowers
    'Mid mountains gloriously arrayed,

2*

Reflecting every brilliant hue
   Of waking dawn, or tranquil eve ;
Whose streams so beautifully blue
   Would oft the stranger's eye deceive,
Who in simplicity ne'er thought
   Such waters could on earth be found,
But deemed them part of yon pure vault,
   Till wakened to their cascade's sound—
Thither to flee, though but to mourn
The loss that saddens our return
May yet console, however late,
The friends that grieve for Rostam's fate."


"Mindah," cried Achmed, smiling, "How
   Couldst thou ignore the soldier's vow?
His plighted honour, glory, fame,
Hope to eternalise his name,
All to his standard firmly bind
His duty, as by heaven assigned ;
Till victory her banner wave
   Before his all delighted eyes ;
Or in his kindred dust—the grave—
   Wept by his country, calm he lies.


" But this rude scene, replete with fear,
   Beseems thee not ; to linger here,
Where deeds of ruthless vengeance bring
Abhorred rebellion on our king,

Were yielding to the vulture's aim
The dove once rescued from the flame.
Herman, who in his lord's defence
   Was wounded in the battle fray,
With strength regained, will guide thee hence,
   And guard thee on thy homeward way.


" I see assembling the divan
   Briefly to ponder measures meet,
Or summon aid from Erivan,
   Or, shame! mayhap, with rebels treat.
I go, though impotent to wield
   The fickle, unreflecting crowd,
At least our sovereign to shield
   From traitor, reckless, false, and proud."


Helmet in hand, he waved adieu
With look so kind, benign, and true,
As all her feelings to inspire
   With hope of future peace;
His courage tried her thoughts admire,
   Her anxious terrors cease.


A youthful maiden, to her call
   Advanced with quiet, mournful pace.
She was of stature slight, not tall,
   Though exquisite in form and face.
Her dark blue eye expressive told
   Of buoyant youth repressed by care;

Circassian born, her locks of gold
    Shaded a front divinely fair,
Her voice from heart of stone or steel
    Fond tears of ecstacy would win,
And all her witching soul reveal
    Responsive to her mandoline—
Whenever thus with kindling eye
She'd breathe a favourite melody.

"Oh! haste to the vale, where the bright flowers are blooming,
    And diamond-like dew drops their beauty adorn;
All grief with the shadow of darkness entombing,
    While the groves wake so sweetly in song to the morn.

" Sure death is not sleep! Oh! no! no! 'tis the waking
    From life's turbid dream, and a long night of pain;
'Tis the day newly born of eternal light breaking,
    That ne'er shall know shadow nor darkness again.

" 'Tis the flight to a region of bliss never-ending,
    Where brighter than diamonds new flowers ever bloom;
Where the sweet notes of rapture from angels attending
    Arise with a triumph of joy o'er the tomb.

" Then weep not as dead, whom the angels are greeting
    With hymns of delight to the bourn of the just;
Shall we mourn! while hope, smiling, e'er points to the meeting
    Kind death will reveal when our embers are dust."

" Flora, thy sweet, consoling strain
    Revives my soul to hope again,
        Though calling forth new tears.

My gentle friend, whence came that **charm**
So soothe, so potent to disarm
   Despondency of fears

" To thee, on life's broad ocean cast,
  The sport of every wayward blast,
    Unsullied by the storm,
I **know** the children of thy soil,
E'er prone to peril and **to toil,**
    Are fraught with feelings **warm.**

" Whene'er to **lute** and **song they list,**
'Tis vain the impulse **to** resist
    That would their thoughts inspire ;
**When** sings the bard of battle won,
Or warlike deed on tyrants done,
    Their very souls are fire.

" But where couldst thou, an exile long,
Attain **that** magic power of song,
    Undisciplined by art ?
To wake, compose, **excite,** or calm—
In the rent bosom pouring balm,
    To heal the wounded heart."

" **Lady,**" said Flora, " Heaven above
Alone bestows the gift you love,
    As once to Jesse's line
The high, immortal power **it** gave ;
But ne'er to tyrant yet, **nor** slave
    Assigned the art divine.

" When torn, in early childhood's years
    From those I loved, with shrieks and tears,
        Far from my native land,
    The dastard Turk, with vengeance foul,
    Exposed me captive at Stamboul,
        In open mart to stand.

" Slave had I been, but pilgrim came
    From Scotia's isle of hallowed fame—³
        Whom childhood's tears detain;
    He tenders gold, his guide commands
    To snatch me from their caitiff hands,
        And loose the galling chain.

" My liberator's happy home
        A charmed asylum gave.
    O'er many a pleasant land we roam,
        And traverse many a wave.
    Blessed with that art beyond his race,
        Deemed by ungifted men a dream:
    In song, his eyes, his aged face
        With saintly joy would beam.

" But when he told of that loved isle,
        His gallant sons defending died,
    With whom heart-rending grief, the while,
        Entombed their mother side by side;
    You'd say no earthly harp could raise
        Notes of that pure, exalted tone,

Commingled with adoring praise
   To that mysterious power alone ;
Who from our deepest pangs can draw
   Our happiness divine, extreme,
Uninfluenced by mortal law,
   Beyond all human thought supreme.

" His plaintive lay impressed my mind
With strange sensation, sad, yet kind ;
His native legends, sweet and wild,
He loved to teach his favoured child—
For such he held me, and esteemed
As blest the Providence that seemed
To doom me to the Moslem's rage,
Yet gave a solace to his age—
Consoling him for those he lost.
What gave him resignation most,
And calmed the anguish of his heart,
Were songs untaught, I learned apart.
Oft would the simple hymn you praise
His very soul to transport raise.

" Impelled by ardent hope, we seek
   Beloved Circassia, there to end
Our varied wandering. But to speak
   Of horrors, they would only tend
To sadden thee ; friends, kindred, gone,
   Our native vale a desert wild,
Of thousands there remained not one
   To mourn the lot of the exiled.

War, plague, or famine's torturing death
   A thorough desolation wrought :
The passing breeze with gentler breath,
    When we in vain the homestead sought,
    Their requiem wailed, I fondly thought.

"My kind protector bade me turn
    While weeping, from the valley's side,
Where plundering Moslems spoil and burn
    Whoe'er could peaceably abide ?
Exclaiming, with a prayer sublime,
   ' Oh, for some earthly region free ;
Some undiscovered, happy clime,
   Exempt from mortal misery,
Unhallowed yet by human crime !'
    O'er rugged mountains thence we haste
In scenes more tranquil to sojourn,
    Remote from home's destructive waste—
Ah ! vain desires all earthly born !

"Tiflis received a weary pair
    Of pilgrims in her friendly towers ;
To which good Herman's anxious care
    Would fain have strewn our path with flowers.
For he had known my guardian long
In distant lands far famed for song.
The blooming isles of Greece were said
To 've had the aged and feeble led
All ardent to admire their lore,
    In conference, from shore to shore.

Even blithesome youth, when **parting day**
Had chased the fervent hours away,
Would oft desert the joyous dance
And yet the pleasing eve enhance,
Illum'd by Dian's silver beam,
Heark'ning to the sage's **theme**;
That pictured empires, states of old
In ancient records rarely **told**—
Retracing generations past,
'Ere war provoked **the trumpet's blast**;
'Ere Delos from the waters sprung,
The Muse inspired, or Homer sung.

" But now the bard's last grief was o'er,
Doomed to adorn the earth no more.
Aware his pilgrimage **was done,**
Meekly his brow with radiance shone.
Those once endeared to him on earth—
Stems of his race, of regal birth,
He said, now beckoned him to come,
And share their bright eternal home.
To Herman charges he assigned
Of jewels—wealth, an ample store,
And the poor orphan he resigned
To faith so tried and proved before.

" I need not say how well the trust
    In that distinguished chief was placed,
Whose wisdom, **provident and** just
    The bitterness of woe effaced;

"For of all favours he could give
    Or bounteous providence could send,
What can compete with this—to live
    Thy cherished, loved, devoted friend?"

"Dear as my life," fair Mindah cried
    And clasped her in her arms the while,
"Friends, orphans, as fond sisters tried
    We'll live though fate may frown or smile."

Lingering o'er such kind embrace
    Angels might gaze with rapture ever;
Tears, soothing grief, bedewed each face,
    With smiles of promise ne'er to sever.

# THE DOOM OF MAC DIARMID,

## An Oriental Legend of the Gael.

### CANTO III.

The war, discursive, sweeps the plain
   And dyes the blushing Zenderud,
That murmuring wafted off the stain,
   As loath to witness human blood.
The shepherd's cot in ruin falls,
   A prey to all-consuming fire;
The peasant sought the city's walls
   Driven by the foe, with fell desire,
That famine might the work of death
   With lighter toil of war achieve,
And plague her pestilential breath
   Condensed evolve, and life bereave.
What fearful shrieks the dead deplore!
   What groans of rage and vengeance mad,
Blent with the gun's alternate roar,
   Boom through the vale of Gulnabad!

An Arab band secured a site
By walls defended, whence they fight

Discharging darts of fatal power
Densely as drops the thunder shower.
Twice repulsed was the hostile line
That boldly dared the barrier mine.
When swift, amid the darts elanced,
Kerman's highland troops advanced—
Then scaled the wall the mountaineer,
To charge the band with sword and spear.

Where was the Arab force could stand
Against the might of Ullah's hand?
Three stalwart brothers of the race
At once his powerful weapon face.
Dashing their pliant spears aside,
From one he draws the purple tide
Out gushing from his wounded throat;
Before another billows float
Crimsoned deep to his closing eyes,
As with cleft brow he prostrate lies.
The third, a youth, disdained to flee
The unequal strife, resolved to be
Victor, or in his visioned heaven
Wrapt in the joys to martyrs given.
His sword breaks short, while that still red
With kindred streams his life blood shed.

" Base offspring of the vandal band,"
    Ullah exclaimed, with glance of scorn,
" Who robbed us of the beauteous land
    Where erst our glorious sires were born;

When Asia bowed beneath their sway,
  And nations their dominion sought,
Which bounteous as the solar ray,
  Gave liberty to life and thought.
All potent Ormusd doomed our sires
—'Wont to depress the world's proud lords
Who desecrate his hallowed fires—
  To yield to such contemptuous hordes."

With frantic grief Abdallah saw
  The bravest of his followers slain,
Like deer beneath the tiger's paw,
  The remnant scattered o'er the plain,
A numerous host, his anxious fears
  Collect them briefly to his aid,
'Till compassed by a grove of spears
  He pointed to the foe and said:
" Sons of the faith will not the sight
  Of Guebre cursed inflame your ire ?
Shall yonder sun's auspicious light
  Behold you flee the slaves of fire ?
'Tis not the Afghan you oppose[1]
  Imbued with our unsullied faith,
But Allah's dire, inveterate foes,
  Foredoomed to Eblis and to death.
Who in the contest falls shall wear
  Immortal laurels : angels wings
His soul to paradise shall bear,
  While the seraphic minstrel sings.
An Houri of celestial charms
Shall smiling fold him in her arms."

His vain prediction could impart
   No pleasure so intensely deep,
As that which lightened Ullah's heart.
   With joy even his associates weep :
For now before them stand arrayed
   The race abhorred, the hated foes,
Who on their homes and altars preyed,
   The long felt cause of all their woes.
With close set teeth, with lips compressed,
   From whence escaped no hostile word ;
Each glance their leader's eye addressed,
   Each hand more tightly grasped the sword.

Speedier than the antelope
   When the wild hunter's darts pursue,
While plunging down the mountain slope,
   O'er blooming heather bright with dew ;
More swiftly than the eagles fly
   To glad with reeking prey their young,
Who in their eyrie perched on high
   Greet them with cries, the rocks among :
Firm and determined rushed the race
Of Kerman's warriors to efface
   The memory of years.
The signal scarce had Ullah given,
Their charge was like the bolt of heaven
   Against the Arab spears.

Dread was the shock, the Moslems reel,
And shudder as the rapid steel

## CANTO III.

 Sweeps down their serried line;
But confidence in numbers, shame,
The all exciting prophet's name,
Their rude desponding souls inflame,
 As sparks the deadly mine.
Their leader turned with fraudful art
His caftan's broidered folds to part;
 Whence secretly he drew
A casket, with dark essence filled
Of concentrated poison stilled,
 His weapon to imbue.

A guard gigantic, stout of heart,
He armed with this envenomed dart,
 And stern injunction gave,
When fiercely raged the combat round,
He should the Sultan Guebre wound,[2]
 And other contests waive;
That Mithra's progeny were charmed,[3]
By spells and incantations armed
 Against assault profane;
But when opposed by weapon given
From sainted Emir, chosen of heaven,
 All magic rites were vain.

Ullah contending in the van,
His gallant followers, man to man,
 Were bathed in hostile blood—
Unconscious, saw with vague surprise
A huge-framed Arab fix his eyes
 On him where'er he stood.

Instinctively his thoughts incline,
To cleave the monster to the spine,
   Who seemed the fight to shun.
When, as the turmoil densely pressed,
The dart was pointed at his breast.'
   To shield him numbers run.
But Ullah's blade with powerful sweep,
Made the empoisoned weapon leap
   Full fifty cubits high,
Whence sheer descending to the earth,
It scarred a youth of noble birth,
   The flower of Araby—
Selim, their leader's son, whose arm
Few yet could ween, encountered harm,
   Curbing his bounding horse;
Till torturing spasm seized the limb—
The face convulsed, the eye waxed dim,
   He fell a blackened corse.


Aghast they view the honored dead,
Who blithely daring at their head,
   Their deep affections won.
Soldiers whose hearts the sire scarce moved
By hope or fear, yet dearly loved
   Abdallah's only son.


Stunned at the sight, to Isfahan,
Confused and horror-struck they ran—
   A few resisting turned;

But strewed the pathway with their slain,
And gasping, wounded, mad with pain,
　　Whom thirst and anger burned.

Rejoiced they ken the city's spires,
Ere Kerman's ardent band retires,
　　Sore wearied with the chase.
For envoys from Mir Maghmud pressed,
With message to their chief addressed,
　　His movement to retrace.
That on his Afghan columns driven,
Sudden as thunderbolt from Heaven,
　　Rushed from an ambuscade,
A party dauntless in the field,
To whom his boldest veterans yield,
　　Entreating Ullah's aid.

　　\*　\*　\*　\*　\*　\*

Screened in a copse beside the stream,
　　That flows by Gulnabad,
Impervious to the noontide beam,
　　Reclined a warrior sad.
'Twas Achmed, while a chosen group
　　Around him lay concealed
Of swiftest steeds, his gallant troop,
　　Within the foliage veiled.
Apart the heir of Persia's throne,
　　Of conquering Abbas sprung,
With Herman communed thus alone,
　　The listless guards among:

" What hope in Isfahan to remain?
 **Where frantic** priests all power control,
 And treason sanctity can feign,
  Abhorrent to the patriot's soul.

" The generous Achmed, whom my sire,
 **By** fanatic Abdallah led,
Aye subjects to the hostile fire,
 Too little recks the carnage **dread.**
Had not thy prudence timely seen
 The covert of this friendly shade,
**Dear** Herman, Persia's prince had **been**
 A victim to the rebel's blade.
But why intently **to yon hill,**
 **So** distant thy regards direct?
Oh! never doubt great Allah will
 Our wayward destiny protect."

" Thæmas, my prince," **Herman replied,**
 " Kind **Providence will e'er** diffuse
**Its** choicest blessings, and abide
 With those who best **its bounties use.**
**Force, intellect, and** sense **were given**
 For action, energy and toil;
Who misapply these gifts of Heaven,
 **Their** future lives of peace despoil.
**Thy** firm resolve to join our band
 Engaged in desperate deeds I praise,
But higher duty calls, the land
 Thou must **to** war's prompt summons **raise.**

" Through the exterior Afghan line,
    That now encompasses our force,
Brave Achmed will, at eve's decline,
    Direct thee with the Georgian horse.
But see that cloud-like vapour rise
    Above the summit of yon mound,
Some smouldering cot in ruin lies,
    The fiends advance—list to the sound!"

Alert, with more attentive ear,
Whence rose the distant smoke, they hear,
Though scarce perceptible at first,
At intervals the warlike burst
Of sounds, that with a deafning roar,
The gale full soon distinctly bore.
Then on the upland crest are seen
The Afghan multitude. I ween
No gallant soldier versed in war,
Viewing their armed array afar,
In fancy's flight, would e'er assign
The downfall of a princely line,
The race of Abbas, Persia's lords,
To such rude, despicable hordes.

So thought at least each Georgian free
As their advancing foes they see,
In scattered masses now descend,
No order keep, nor ranks attend;
No vanguard mark their destined course—
Horse mixed with foot, and foot with horse.

Herman observed—made fully known
His plans to Achmed, then alone
Privily to Gulnabad retired,
Whose strong defence new hope inspired.
Meantime, within the copse's range,
The prince and Achmed arms exchange;
That Thæmas safely might, disguised,
Proceed as Herman had advised.

In Maghmud's army were enrolled
Some troops of Tartars, brave and bold,
Who, when on distant wars retained,
Their patient camels daily trained [5]
To bear huge guns, and promptly kneel
At signal, word, or touch of steel,
With necks decumbent to the ground,
Till from their burthened backs a round
Of this rude ordnance was discharged;
Nor were the gentle brutes enlarged,
Till day, departing in the west,
Proclaimed the grateful hour of rest.

With vaunting clamour, on they come,
Shrill sounds the trumpet, rolls the drum.
In hopes of many a glittering prize
Their shouts ascended to the skies.
While Maghmud from the van withdraws,
Commanding an immediate pause.

In Gulnabad no cry is heard,
No sign of soldier armed appeared,
   Yet still suspicion rose;

## CANTO III.

Her walls a force might safely screen,
Most formidable though unseen,
   Of stern, determined foes.

The camels to the front were brought,
When from the cannon's iron throat,
   A volley dense was fired.
Some roofs were shattered; columns tall
And spires were seen in dust to fall,
   Ere the report expired.
Then rigid silence seemed to reign,
As in a desolate domain—
   The Afghan chiefs rejoice;
For barbarous soldiers ever bent
To crowd with useless spoil the tent,
   Heed not a leader's voice.

They enter, emulous in toil,
The splendid palaces to spoil,
   That Gulnabad adorn;
Till court-yard, alley, terrace, street,
With ruffian hordes were half replete,
   By thirst of plunder borne.

Then rose a cry of dread surprise,
As, dazzling their bewildered eyes,
Volley on volley quickly flies,
   From latticed tower and hall.
Vainly they call on Allah's name,
Stones seem to gape and vomit flame,
Whence shot and darts as deadly came,
   Their boldest veterans fall.

Confused and terrified they fly,
Anxious to seek for covert nigh,
While, heaps on heaps, their bravest die,
   Entreating aid in vain.
A marble passage, arched and wrought
With texts of Koran, numbers sought—
Some for its shelter madly fought,
   While bullets poured like rain.

Herman, who in a mosque had staid,
To which the marbled archway led,
Now, smiling, to his soldiers said,
   "Heaven prospers our design."
A train beneath the archway ended,
From the guarded mosque extended,
Here with lighted brand he wended
   And fired a secret mine.

Astounding was the loud uproar,
While columns with their bases soar,
And mangled members drenched in gore,
   Like rockets poised in air.
Horrified, appalled, amazed,
Deep stupor on the Afghans seized,
They thought the flames of Eblis blazed,
   In light and thunder there.

Recoiling with instinctive fear,
Impeding obstacles they clear,
And curse the spoil, no longer dear,
   That tempted their desire.

Retreating from the fatal walls,
Obedient to their leader's calls,
Many a victim prostrate falls
   Beneath the scattering fire.

The Afghan chiefs to Maghmud came,
Conjuring him, by Mirvais' fame,
To cross in force the ruddy stream,
   And seize a neighbouring brae
Commanding Gulnabad, and crown
With guns the summit, thence pour down
Their fire on the devoted town,
   And its defenders slay.
The thought converts despair to joy.
Ever most eager to destroy,
He bade his soldiers rafts employ
   To cross the swollen flood;
For high and broad the waters rose,
Sudden, from late dissolving snows
On distant mountains, whence it flows,
   The beauteous Zenderud.

The pioneers, with lusty call
Apply the axe, assistants haul,
Trees of an hundred ages fall,
   Loud crashing, to the ground.
The camels, from the guns untied,
They gently to the margin guide;
The horsemen through the torrent ride;
   The beaten waves resound.

Achmed perceived with anxious heart
   The thundering of the blasted mine :
The Afghans, terrified, depart
   And to the stream their force incline.
He then addresses Persia's heir :
   " Most noble prince, now haste with those
Two Georgian chiefs, who'll safely bear
   Thee far beyond thy ruthless foes ;
Advance securely through the glade,
Veiled by the trees' protecting shade,
But on the unincumbered plain,
Ply well the spur, and loose the rein.
Pass not the river till a mound,
   A ford adjoining, meets your view—
By foes this morn 'twas guarded round,
   Now safe the path you may pursue ;
No Afghan outposts tarry there,
   The scouts who have remarked it tell ;
Return with speed ; till conquest fair
   Shall Persia liberate—farewell."

With sad regret the prince departs,
Veiling the friendly tear that starts,
   For Achmed he admired ;
Whose fate must hazard all, he knew,
Who ne'er with forces weak nor few,
   From threat'ning foe retired.

Mir Maghmud's cavalry attain
A wide-spread field, a beauteous plain
   That stretched from hill to grove.

## CANTO III.

The hill they sought with so much zeal,
The grove where Achmed's troops conceal
Their presence for the prince's weal,
   Whose friendship gained their love.

Impatiently the Moslem horse
Direct their unimpeded course
   To seize the rising ground;
To wait for infantry they scorn,
Who failed to pass the stream till borne
   On rafts together bound.
Fervent in rivalry they fly
Eager to gain its summit high,
   When numbers disappeared;
Deep pits had caved its sloping side,
By boughs and light earth covered wide,
That sharpened stakes completely hide,
   Where man and horse are speared.

Then came a storm with brilliant sheen
From breastwork, hitherto unseen,
   Of grape-shot and Greek fire.
The horseman, with a languid moan,
The horse, with wild unearthly groan,
   In torturing pangs expire.
The remnant, in dismay, recede
To where the infantry, with speed,
   Now raft the current o'er,
And joining prudently each flank
Of troops now landed on the bank,
   Assail the hill once more.

Oh! who can Achmed's followers blame,
When brightly burned the battle flame,
And war's deep sounds in thunder came,
  For one indignant thought?
That prudence more than just retained
Their leader brave, when might be gained
A glorious field; they scarce refrained
  Their passion, overwrought.

But now with joy their hearts expand,
As Achmed calmly gave command
That each should by his courser stand,
  Armed and prepared to ride;
That, from the grove once cleared away,
No warrior from his rank should stray,
But in the hottest of the fray
  His signal well abide.

As with grave energy he spoke,
The gale dispelled the battle smoke,
  When on the hill is seen—
Although no hand appeared to move—
Rising the well-fought field above,
  A banner gold and green.

Achmed, with quiet, meaning smile,
Upvaulted on his steed the while—
  A gift the prince bestowed;
Then to his soldiers passed the sign
To mount, advance, and form their line,
  When through the copse they rode.

## CANTO III.

As from the grove the band emerged,
Downward the brunt of battle **verged,**
   And centred in the plain.
**The** Afghans standing not the flash
**Of** ordnance, while the kuzzlebash [6]
Oft on their lines resistless dash,
   And then retire again.

Twice foiled, they **would** have fled, **but most**
Expected aid from Maghmud's **host,**
   When landed from the stream.
**Why pause the** host **of Candahar?**
Come they alert from realms afar
   On battle field to dream?
They linger on the banks amazed,
**Struck** with terror, as they gazed,
For brightly in the sunlight blazed,
   The Georgian sword and spear.
**Trebly their** awe augmented, **since**
**They** deemed they saw **proud** Persia's **prince**
**Lead as to** make their warriors wince,
   And pale **with abject fear.**

Like lambent fire in their veins
A wild impulsive ardor reigns
Through Achmed's force, that nought restrains,
   Their very souls enlarge,
**As on** Mir Maghmud's heartless crowd,
Elate they hear, distinct and loud,
Their leader's order calm and proud,
   " Quick time, advance and charge."

As prone the golden harvest lithe
Beneath the urgent reaper's scythe,
So falls of Maghmud's force a tithe
   Beneath the Georgian sword;
While thousands to the river hie,
And back the rafts more quickly ply.
All for the safe enjoyments sigh
   Their native vales afford.
Some plunged into the turbid wave
Hoping their dastard lives to save.
A few, resisting, vainly brave,
   A death more noble found.
Fear urged them downward to the stream,
Above them spears and sabres gleam,
Who durst not bide the glancing beam
   Are in the torrent drowned.

Amid the surging waters rushed
The Georgian horsemen, heated, flushed;
Wounds from their glimmering weapons gushed
   In rills of hostile gore.
The stream they would have passed, and fought
The crowded foe who safety sought,
In further flight by panic wrought,
   But Achmed cried "No more!"

He had marked, when issuing from the wood,
How doubtful still the contest stood,
   Where Herman's Persian force,

Descending from the hill, had made
Assaults repeated and essayed
To conquer numbers, well arrayed,
    Of infantry and horse.
He bade his gallant troop retire
From the red stream; their martial fire
    Is but excited more,
As bounding on the plain-they see
The dubious scale of victory,
Now wavering, verge more partially
    The rebel standard o'er.

Impressed with far superior might
The Afghans struggled in the fight,
    Supposing aid at hand;
The sounds, that from the stream they hear,
Bespoke they thought Mir-Maghmud near,
    With hosts at his command.

Who can describe their fell despair
At Achmed thundering on their rear,
Loath, though of gentle heart, to spare
    A rebels forfeit blood?
Less prone to pity, rushed his men
Like lions famished from their den
To raze the careful shepherd's pen,
    In mountain, moor, or wood.

Confounded and bereft of aid,
The rebel wings no more delayed
To fight, where numbers lowly laid
    Betokened their defeat.

With battered armour, wearied steed,
Wounds that at every motion bleed,
No more of battle's toil they heed,
   But, foiled again, retreat.

Then might be seen from hill to stream,
By the mild evening sun's red beam,
   The relics of the fight—
The sloping hill with dead bestrewed—
An Afghan party here pursued,
For none the combat fierce renewed,
   But wished the coming night.
Some to the grove for safety fled,
Whose deepening shade a covert spread—
   Some further haunts explore.
Vast numbers to the river pressed,
By thirst, fatigue, and heat distressed,
And in its cooling waves immersed,
   Plunge deep, to rise no more.

At length night's sable wings o'ershield
The fugitive, and dim the field;
While stars, unnumbered, beam from heaven,
To orbs more grateful kindly given.
Faint was their light, reflected here
From shattered helm and broken spear,
As if their pure beams paled to read
Man's frantic ire and ruthless deed;
They called the breeze of night between
To cloud the page, obscure the scene.

The night wind came, but brought no cloud
To wrap the fallen in peaceful shroud;
But sighing gently as it rose,
Allured the world to calm repose;
And then in solemn stillness shed
Its dewy tear-drops o'er the dead.

# THE DOOM OF MAC DIARMID,

## An Oriental Legend of the Gael.

### CANTO IV.

Shiraz in splendour once outvied [1]
    All cities of the East;
Her domes of porphyry rose in pride,
    Her halls for kings to feast.
How gloriously her temple soared
    With light exalted spire,
Where consecrated priest had stored
    The bright perpetual fire.
Rose-perfumed was the ambient air;
    Cool streams from mountain snow
Basked in the brilliant sunbeams there,
    And soothed their ardent glow.
Well might her shrines superb, her towers,
    Columns ornate in gold,
Her terraced gardens, groves and bowers,
Her luscious fruit, her peerless flowers
    Elysian charms unfold.

Heaven exiled Peris, poets sing,
    A home on earth could ne'er abide,
'Till bounteous Summer, budding Spring,
In pity to the wandering,
    Shiraz fair stream on either side,
With roses culled from Eden clad—
The winsome banks of Rocknabad.[2]

Ill-omened hour! the spoiler came
With force destructive, 'till her name
    Alone survived the blight ;
The rude Arabian, tribe and horde,
Vulture-like on her people poured,
    And conquered in the fight.

Though fanatic and frenzied zeal
Their faith to speed, by force of steel,
    The hostile cause sustained ;
No treason foul, nor impious fraud[3]
Their sanguinary deeds outlawed,
    Nor reckless courage stained.

Not so when Persia owned their sway,
    And luxury engendered pride,
Intestine war, remorseless fray,
    And treachery their faith belied.
The chieftain by his sovereign raised
    To wealth, distinction, power, and fame,
His envied dignities erased,
    Exulting in a traitor's name.

## CANTO IV.

Isfahan, deep thy people felt[4]
   Treason's abhorred, infernal art;
While prostrate in their shrines they knelt,
   No ruth assailed Abdallah's heart.
By bribes and hopes of future power,
   Mir Maghmud sought his impious aid;
He yields, and in one fatal hour,
   His country's sacred cause betrayed.

Implore not on the traitor's head
Ill fate or malediction dread,
   Man's imprecations fail.
But heaven's high will, mysterious seeming,
The patriot and the just redeeming,
   Annihilates his weal,
Corrodes his heart with sickening throes,
His bosom robs of bland repose,
   And wrecks his tortured brain;
Converts his thoughts to black despair,
Repelling hope, implanting care
   And agonizing pain;
Removing all that held him dear,
With all he loved and cherished here,
   Commuting friend to foe;
And raising to his gaze when late,
And prostrate fallen, his future fate—
   Eternity of woe.

In mourning groups the mosque they leave,
And anxious hurry to receive

Wild tidings, that obscurely told
How Achmed and his Georgians bold
Encountering—at the Zenderud—
Repulsed Mir Maghmud o'er the flood;
That Persia's princely heir secure
    Had passed unharmed the hostile lines,
And hastened levies to ensure
    Destruction to the foe's designs.
A ray of hope its influence shed,
    That Isfahan might yet be saved,
Though plague could count her thousands dead,
    And all relief from famine craved.


Along the shady meidan moved
    Mindah and Flora arm in arm;
Right dearly were they prized and loved,
    Their deeds diffused so sweet a charm.
They sought the wounded and infirm,
    Daily their bounteous gifts to share,
Regardless from infecting germ
    Of pestilence their lives to spare.
Mindah was pleased that fame had spread
Her envied wreaths o'er Achmed's head;
Flora, resigned to sorrow, sighed
That human hearts to heaven allied
Should their high destiny degrade,
By baneful war's unhallowed aid.
Both saddened as the fruits they see—
Grief, death, disease and misery.

## CANTO IV.

A mother frantic, pale and wild,
   With famine on her cheek impressed,
Besought them to restore her child,
   She held half lifeless to her breast.
She said her husband late had gone,
   When ordered, to the battle field;
But wounded, faint, returned alone,
   Wanting the aid she could not yield.
To her unhappy home they hie,
   With means restorative prepared,
Where still and death-like seemed to lie
   A soldier of Abdallah's guard.


Some drops of renovating power
   And virtue to his lips applied
By Flora's hand, his sense restore,
   Though tremors in his limbs abide.
With nutrient balm and Shiraz wine
   Mindah the wife and babe revives:
They deemed that Allah's hand divine
   Had angels brought to guard their lives.


The soldier starts, as from a trance,
At Mindah's kind enquiring glance,
And with augmented shuddering cries,
" Lady, avert those awful eyes,
Whose mild though superhuman light
Recalls the terrors of the fight,

When raging on our front and wing
Rushed Kerman's bands.   Their Guebre king,
   Embayed, I sought to wound;
The lightnings from his eyes that part,
Like thine, though fierce, enerved my heart
   In fear and horror bound.
His glance and sword avert the blow,
The dart, I'm wont to surely throw,
   Another victim found,
Selim the brave, our army's pride—
Whom racked in torture I'd have died
   With joy to shield from harm—
Fell prostrate, an unseemly corse;
I wot not by the weapon's force
   But Guebre's magic charm.

" Abandoned since to want and grief,
Reduced to hope an exit brief
   By death from famine's sting;
'Till by your kind auspicious care
Allah is pleased our lives to spare,
   And soothing comfort bring."

Colchian mines were rich in ore,
Oman's sea pure pearls bore;
Full argosies, at every breeze,
Ploughed deep the purple Indian seas
   Designed for Persia's court.
O'er mountain oft and waste of sand,
Would caravan through Samarcand
   To Isfahan resort:

## CANTO IV.

There shone the brillant coral stem,
The diamond bright, the sparkling gem,
 At many a regal fete;
When peace her myrtle wreathed above,
Proclaiming harmony and love,
 With happiness replete.
But all the treasures earth could give
 In orient splendor dight,
Where pride and foul ambition live
 Conduce not to delight;
Could not in gentle Mindah's heart
A solace to her grief impart.
 Far dearer than all these
The signs of gratitude that teem
For life restored, in eyes that beam.
Oh! joy unuttered to redeem
 War's doleful miseries.

With tender interest they explore
The unsought dwellings of the poor,
What recent sufferers diseased
Famine and plague combining seized.
'Twas woe to see the number vast,
On their rough couches helpless cast—
Wounded, hungered, fevered, raving,
Last adieus to kindred waving;
Yet even the dying smiled to see
The votaries of charity,
In gentlest tone, their wants enquire,
 Palliate their torturing pain.

With cool sherbet assuage the fire,
   That fiercely burned the anguished brain.

Well was the lore the pilgrim **bard**
   On his adopted child bestowed.
From Flora's prescience and regard
   To threatened danger blessings **flowed**.
**Refined in culinary art,**
   The choicest beverage she elects ;
With kindness acts the nurse's **part—**
   With prayer implores, with smile directs.

**Wounded, by weight of age oppressed,**
**Great Merdan lay devoid of rest.**
**Infirmity and pain combine**
To **herald death's** approaching sign.
With bosom tranquil, thoughts sedate,
Resigned like martyr to his fate,
He bade his treasured gold be brought
And the devoted **sisters sought**
To utilize **the plenteous store,**
   Relieving want, disease and **sorrow,**
**His days of** toil **on earth were o'er,**
   While loomed in darkning doubt his morrow.

Flora entreated he'd allow
   Her nursing care to tend his **age,**
Appease the thirst and cool the brow,
   The wounds with anodynes assuage.
" No, beauteous maid !" the veteran cried,
   With languid voice, " **Thy noble aim**

Could not, with all that art supplied
    Restore this frail exhausted frame.
But sing to me ; thy voice will charm,
    And by its melody recall
The days of youth, when passion warm—
    For warlike fame enraptures all."

Resigned, in melancholy mood
    Flora the vocal art essayed,
Grieved that his thoughts should ne'er allude
    To heaven's benign, all-powerful aid.

" The land was invaded, the bard took the sword,
And flew to the shrine where her people adored.
There crowded with ardor the bold and the brave,
Their homes and their altars, their freedom to save.
He points to the valley, the field, and the grove,
The scene of their childhood, their toil, and their love ;
To the grave of their sires they were wont to revere,
And implored them to enter the battle with prayer.

" With cheerful compliance they march to the field—
The minstrel their leader, but Heaven was their shield.
The sound of the war song enhanced their delight,
As with transport they charge in the storm of the fight.
They thought not of laurels, they recked not of lives,
Defending their country, their homesteads and wives.
At the foeman's proud hosts would the timid despair,
'Till remembering, they breathed in mute fervor a prayer.

" Outnumbered and wearied, yet fearlessly all
Were contending when thunder clouds suddenly fall ;
While blasts from the northward incessantly blow,
With lightning and hail in the face of the foe.

" Resistance is conquered, the battle is o'er ;
　The free shall regard an invader no more.
　From the victors with heads to the lightning laid bare
　Amid trumpets resounding, ascended the prayer."

　　　Memory lights the veteran's eye,
　　　　To ecstacy his spirit rose,
　　　And murmuring prayer and victory,
　　　　Dissolved in placid calm repose.

　　　\*　　　\*　　　\* .　　　\*　　　\*

　　　A wailing sound of sorrow came
　　　　The city's pallid crowds among,
　　　Fanned by the voice of erring fame,
　　　　Or from designing treason sprung,
　　　That Ullah, joined with Maghmud's host,
　　　　Fair Gulnabad had stormed and burned.
　　　Rumour detailed that all was lost,
　　　　Their prince impeded had returned.

　　　Advancing with portentous speed,
　　　Was seen his fiery, coal-black steed.
　　　His arms shone brightly from afar,
　　　As swift he sought the Chilminar.
　　　Yet much they marveled, as he rode,
　　　How gallantly his barb he strode,
　　　That flying like the sea-bird home,
　　　Curved the proud neck, bestarred with foam.
　　　The palace won, the gates unfold
　　　　To yield him prompt admittance there :
　　　None born on earth, 'twas thought, so bold
　　　　E'er entered thus, but Persia's heir.

## CANTO IV.

\* \* \* \*

Reclining in her bower of ease,
Forced by fatigue from toil to cease,
Mindah her wealth computed o'er,
Her gems and gold—a bounteous store,
That all might be diffused at need,
The famished multitude to feed;
Grieving to contemplate how small
The aid, distributed to all;
Her cheek, alternate pale and red,
The holier light her dark eyes shed,
Invincible resolve declare,
Their misery she felt bound to share.

Issuing from a trellised grove,
   Voices her reverie refrain,
That praised her deeds, but interwove
   Sad fears of peril and of pain.
Advancing forth with anxious air,
   Lo! Achmed, prince-like, still disguised,
With Flora, from her daily care
   Of duties, so beloved and prized.

"Welcome, dear Achmed," Mindah cried,
   "But why that jewelled turban wear?
Couldst thou, who on the cross relied,
   Thy faith for empires here forswear?
Can that gold crescent be the meed
   Our dear loved chieftain's valour bought?
Sad emblem of the moslem creed;
   I tremble at the impious thought.

Abandon the unholy sign,
  The Christian soldier should forego,
That suffering in the truth divine,
  Hope may embalm our tears of woe."

" Believe not that the outward dress
  Can indicate the soul's impress.
  No, Mindah, star of all that's good,
  'Twas donned to save the prince's blood,
  Who in the Georgian's plain attire,
  By prudent Herman's sage desire,
  Is now amassing friends afar,
  To stem the sanguined tide of war ;
  Needless their tardy help, I trust,
  For Maghmud's bravest in the dust
  We hope to prostrate, e'er yon sun
  Another day's bright period run.

" Already, winged by fear they fled
    Beyond the reach of Georgian spears ;
  But rallied by the gallant head
    Of Kerman's hardy mountaineers,
  They readvance in force complete,
    And burning with indignant shame,
  A glorious chance in fight to meet
    Those Guebres of distinguished fame.
  Meantime I haste with speed to bring,
    At Herman's need, a powerful train
  Of ordnance, granted by the king,
    Ere Gulnabad be stormed again.

## CANTO IV.

" But why that melancholy sigh ?
   Those sounds of sorrow rend thy heart,
The widow's shriek, the orphan's cry—
   Dear Mindah thou shouldst hence depart,
With escort suited to o'ercome
   The foe's most threatening powers ;
Full soon we'll follow, victors home,
   To Tiflis' friendly towers."


" No Achmed, save with thee to fly
All ties of duty power deny.
While thou our country's cause defend,
'Tis mine to act the soldier's friend,
What aid shall Georgia's wounded find
If Rostam's heir that charge resigned ?
When friends from kindred separate,
By famine's pangs consigned to fate,
And hecatombs of victims rise,
To deadly plague a sacrifice ;
We hope the grief to palliate
   Of ills we cannot all remove ;
Flora, my sister, known too late,
   Joins in the task with ardent love.
While her more learned art attains
   Abatement of the dire disease,
I go where raging famine reigns,
   Rejoiced to make the monster cease.
Such foes are worthy of our zeal,
   Whom arms of steel could ne'er subdue ;

Deluded man the truth should feel
    And war like **ours alone** pursue.

" But Achmed, should **thine** ardour bring,
    Or incident of battle urge
Thine arm against the Guebre king,
    The wretched Moslem's dreaded scourge;
**Remember in the wars of old,**
    When **Rostam**, captive in the strife,
Was brought **to Cloghan's** mountain **hold**
    He gave **him** liberty and life.
**With grateful** kindness then prevent
    **His doom from** any Georgian sword,
**Who mournfully with us** lament
    Their good, their venerated lord.

" When roars the battle thou mayest see
    Some unarmed suppliant pity crave ;
Spare life in memory of me,
    Heaven loves the **bountiful and** brave.
And shouldst **thou yet** unharmed return,
    **To find thine own** betrothed **no more**
Do not, dear Achmed, deeply mourn,
    Nor vain, fond hopes on earth deplore."

Her diamond girdle she withdrew
    With strange and mystic symbol **traced,**
A pearly **tear** bedimmed her view,
    While on his breast **the** cross she placed.
She said 'twas thought to have the power,
    By saints of old, and prophets **given,**

## CANTO IV.   65

To shield the good in danger's hour,
   Or raise the wandering thought to Heaven.
She begged her Achmed ne'er to part
   The gift her childhood loved to save;
But aye preserve it near his heart,
   When wildflowers blossomed on her grave.


So mild and sweet, though sad her tone,
Inspired a feeling pure and lone,
Partaking less of mundane love
Than that of angels throned above.


Achmed, a while entranced in sense,
Stood mute in statue-like suspense.
His brow revealed an inward pain,
As feeling utterance strove to gain.
" Mindah, sole treasure of my heart,
   Pure light of Georgia's smiling home,
Bid not thy soldier hence depart,
   With awe foreboding ills to come.


" A panoply of justice shields
   The warrior faithful to his trust,
To whom the fierce invader yields,
   Or dies resisting in the dust.
As sacred as the ruby tide
   That heaves thy pulse, that warms thy breast,
Shall Kerman's king in safety bide,
   Should we the gallant chief arrest.

"But thou thy toil, sweet princess, spare,
  Howe'er so hallowed, 'tis not well
To frequent haunts infected, where
  Dire misery and contagion dwell.
Oh! cease thy fond solicitude
  To tend the wretched day by day.
But hark! the trumpet's sound, though rude,
  To duty calls, I must away."

A look of parting anguish flew
From tearful eyes. A faint adieu
Breathed from the purest hearts that e'er
At incensed altar offered prayer.

# THE DOOM OF MAC DIARMID,

## An Oriental Legend of the Gael.

### CANTO V.

Changed are Mir Maghmud's bold designs.
Taught by repulse, he closed his lines
Nearer the city, to restrain
All ingress from the fertile plain;
And forming camps defensive, tried
The issue of the war to bide,
'Till dearth called forth her people's cries,
And Isfahan fell his glorious prize.

Pacing his solitary tent,
   The varied fortune of his race
Struck Ullah's heart, in anguish bent;
   Dejection marked the warrior's face.
Convinced as taught, when earth-born men
   Sprung forth from dust at Heaven's command,
That Mithra's line more sacred then,
   Were formed express by Ormusd's hand,
To govern with exalted sway
   Empires and kingdoms of the earth;

Alas! their thrones have passed away
    To recreants of ignoble birth;
And, bitter thought! to raze his home
    'Mid solitudes remote and wild,
Where freedom dwelt, foes dared to come
    And murder parent, wife, and child.

To boundless grief succeeds a thirst
    For vengeance on the ruthless powers
Of Arab plunderers, who durst
    Fire his unguarded native towers;
But chiefly on the bigot king
    Of Abbas' proud, detested blood,
From whose vile sway such evils spring,
    Like torrents from a mountain flood.

While luridly the watchfire blazed
The awning of his tent was raised.
A stranger entered, humbly clad,
Dervise-like, robed in raiment sad.
But when emerging from the shade,
The rays upon his features played,
Kind Herman's aspect they reveal—
Replete with thought, resolved though pale.

The Guebre Ullah gazed with dread,
As on a spirit from the dead;
Yet more his awe and wonder grew,
    When Herman the dark robe displaced,
And from beneath the folds withdrew
    A scroll with mystic symbols traced.

## CANTO V.

"Speak! speak! cried Ullah, hast thou come
 Commissioned from a higher sphere,
Or hast thou 'scaped the sanguined doom
 When sought in battle at my spear?
The sacred symbols of a race,
 Now fall'n, thou bearest, whence com'st thou,
 [say?"

"I come a messenger of peace,
 List patient, noble prince, I pray;
When Cloughan where ye reigned as lords
Was fired by vagrant Arab hordes;
Rostam, intent on friendship's calls,
Was journeying to your highland halls;
Descrying from a distant mound
The fearful blaze, the startling sound,
He rushed to save, should aught remain
As yet unscathed, though small his train.

"Thy people shuddered when he came
 Attempting to subdue the flame;
'Avaunt! 'tis sacrilege,' they cry,
Then instant horror-stricken fly,
Boding disaster on his head
Who dared to combat fire so dread,[1]
That from their hallowed shrine was spread.

"Foiled in the elemental strife,
 He ventured all to rescue life.
A palace near the shrine was raised,
Whose roof with red effulgence blazed;

While from a lattice, where the heat
Had caused her trembling to retreat,
A babe, whose bloom three Summers warmed,
Appeared to cling, he saw alarmed,
And through the smouldering portal flew—
The chamber gained, the babe withdrew.
Yet while he leaves the tottering walls,
The roof a smoking ruin falls.

"The Georgian suite admire the child,
Whose charms, angelic, pure and mild,
Seemed through her tearful eyes to beam
That witnessed the devouring flame;
In which she deemed her all involved,
And every tie on earth dissolved.
A jewelled zone her person graced
   With the same characters inwrought,
That on this scroll are clearly traced,
   A bard from foreign kingdoms brought."

With desperate effort on his part
To still the beating of his heart
Ullah exclaimed, "Pray Georgian tell
What destiny that babe befell;
Soon blighted in her tender bloom,
Hath fate consigned her to the tomb?"

"Grief nearly closed her infant years;
   At Tiflis long she wept and mourned,
'Till soothing time assuaged her tears,
   When florid health to youth returned.

CANTO V.       71

Her feature, manner, form, and grace,
Proclaim her kin to Ullah's race;
Such queen-like dignity enhanced
Her native charms, as years advanced.

"Once tidings strange to Georgia came,
    That Kerman's chief at Candahar,
When Cloughan's walls were wrapt in flame,
    Was pondering private schemes of war—
That, versed in subtle, foul, intrigue,
    Mirvais by fraud designed to bring
Kerman's brave warriors in a league
    With traitors to oppose the king.
Through agents whom the just would spurn,
    He had subornèd Arab tribes,
Men outlawed, thy retreat to burn,
    Bound secretly by oaths and bribes.

"Attachment to the child impelled
Our prince, although his heart rebelled,
To send even to the traitor's den,
So frequented by hostile men,
A special envoy to enquire
If Ullah knew of Mindah's sire,
Or if the orphan's friends survived.
Alas! the mission ne'er arrived.
The faithful envoy's corse was found,
    His garments stiff with gore congealed;
Murdered, he fell on Afghan ground—
    A vaunting priest the truth revealed.

As if the crime, by Heaven abhorred,
Were grateful to his Moslem lord.

"Dear as an heir and daughter loved,
  The orphan, since that fatal day
Worthy of Rostam's kingdom proved;
  And now fair Georgia owns her sway."

With rapture thrilled, though gushing tears
  Bedewed stern Ullah's manly face,
"Pardon," he cried, "our frantic fears,
  Great Ormusd, guardian of our race.
One blossom to adorn the stem
  Thou hast preserved in Ullah's line—
One pure, one solitary gem,
  My Mindah! daughter! all that's mine."

"You owe" quoth Herman humbly, "yet
Of gratitude a deeper debt,
To Him whose providential care
Would even in flames thy kindred spare.

"Long, long ere Greece her conquests spread,
And steel-armed hosts to Persia led,
Who in thine ancient annals versed,[2]
Knows not what glory in the west
Adorned a branch of Mithra's race,
Renowned in war, beloved in peace?
That line extinct thy nation deems,
  But destiny's mysterious ways

Educed a scion thence that seems
   Worthy of Iran's proudest days."

**Awful**, incredulous surprise
**Beamed** from the Guebre's wondering eyes,
And marked the pausing, faltering sound
Demanding in a voice profound,
" **What knowest** thou of that branch renowned ?"

" List, chief of Kerman, you shall **hear**
   The fortune of the noblest seer
   That e'er adorned thy kingly line,
   Whose lineage you may best define.

" **Some twenty** Summers past **there came,**
    Where exiled princes oft resort,
Diarmid, a wanderer known to fame,
   To Tiflis' hospitable court.
A dignity, a princely mien,
   Profound, even superhuman lore
Proved what vicissitudes he'd seen,
   And treasured in his memory bore.
That skill in harmony divine,[3]
   Revealed to ancient Greece alone,
**To** him did Providence **assign,**
   Though **else to all the world unknown.**
**His sons** their **country's cause** maintained,
   And armed for freedom, martyrs died ;
**Save one, a** tender youth remained
   His consolation and his **pride.**

It grieved the anxious parent's heart,
    The youth should yield his soul to arms,
So alien to the gentle art
    Of song, inspiring heavenly charms."

"That boy's devotion I'd admire,"
Quoth Ullah," if the martial fire
Thus kindling in a youthful soul
Could e'er his future path control.
When helpless nations wronged complain,
And bold usurping tyrants reign,
Arms should delight the brave and free
More than the sweetest minstrelsy.
Oh! the hard fate that aye denied
The blessing of a son," he sighed—
Yet with desponding, anxious heed,
Urged Herman pausing, to proceed.

"In foreign wars, as Rostam knew,
    Georgia might future glory gain;
He sought the youth, so brave, so true,
    On battle field in arms to train.
Inured to misery by the past,
    Like ore in furnaces refined,
Diarmid his cherished, dearest, last
    And sole surviving boy resigned:
Then to his wanderings turned alone,
    And yet not solitary seemed,
The creatures that his mind had grown
    Consoled, and half his pangs redeemed.

"Again we met, where Ilion's site
    Small record of the fame displays
Of kings and heroes fall'n in fight,
    Still living in the poet's lays.
O'er the enchanting shores and isles
    I travelled, by the wanderer led,
Where nature in profusion smiles,
    And Homer toiled in vain for bread.
The land that once Cambyses gained,
    By conquering arms and seas of gore,
His deep research so long detained—
    We parted as to meet no more.

"Twelve years elapsed, the son had grown
    A warlike chief at Tiflis court,
As Achmed or Mac Diarmid known,
    In tournament or princely sport.

"One Summer's eve, so mild and calm,
    When slept the breeze replete with balm;
The odour from the wild flowers' breath
    Pervaded mountain, field, and grove,
Entrancing sense; 'twould lighten death,
    Luring our hope to joys above.
While musing in a vale, apart
From Tiflis' gaily crowded mart,
A message of strange import said
An aged friend, believed as dead,
To rest his wearied limbs had come
Beneath our humble, friendly dome.

"There Diarmid lay, but nought repined
  His strength exhausted, for his mind !
  If human thought e'er soared sublime
  Through boundless space, or endless time,
  Worthy of provident regard,
  'Twas that of the immortal bard.

"Methought the care divine was proved,
  Ere death his peaceful soul removed;
  For watching o'er his couch there seemed
  A maid, whose eyes ecstatic beamed
  With fond attention, filial love,
  Hallowed as that of saints above ;
  Of noble birth, Circassian born,
    Chains had her infant limbs defiled ;
  When Diarmid in her life's young morn
    Adopted her a favourite child.
  And Flora well his bounty paid
    By acts of tenderness and care;
  His home a heaven on earth she made,
    And charmed his thoughts to linger there.

"The bard lamented oft his son
  On warlike expedition gone,
  And hoped that, casting arms aside,
  He'd win fair Flora for his bride.
  Her voice the wild desire might tame
  Of transitory human fame ;
  For much he feared an early tomb
  By fate of war was Achmed's doom.

# CANTO V.

" Among the various gifts bequeathed
    His son and the Circassian maid,
This scroll was found, with signs inwreathed,
    Within a jewelled casket laid.
Now mark, brave Ullah, Kerman's lord,
    Those symbols I before thee place
Comprise a name by all adored,
    And designate an ancient race ;
That once o'er Iran ruled supreme,
    The pride and glory of the land,
Endowed with peace a happy realm,
    And thrones subdued to her command.
Descended from that regal line
    Is Achmed, noble Diarmid's son,
And if we trust to mystic sign
    Achmed's and Mindah's race are one.
The diamond zone that decked her breast,
    When young and rescued from the fire,
Contains those characters impressed,
    Which mark the race of Achmed's sire."

Ullah intent the scroll surveys [4]
Suspended in a lambent blaze,
And when ignited from the flame,
Immersed it in a limpid stream ;
Whence raising it upon his spear,
The symbols still more bright appear ;
With others hitherto unseen,
Shining above, below, between,
Signs of a language lost or dead.
In joy subdued he calmly read :

"Sacred to the glorious line
　Descended from a source divine,
　By Ormusd, in their natal hour,[5]
　Crowned with Iran's sovereign power;
　To rule in peace the land for ever,
　　'Till kindred ties be rent away,
　'Till impious pride their concord sever,
　　'Till time expire, or Mithra's ray
　Their feud on battle field discover;
　　Angels on high were heard to say
　　　'CHILDREN OF AMITA,[5]
　　　HALLOWED IN UNITY,
DESPOT OR DEMON SHALL CONQUER YOU NEVER.'"

Herman approached with solemn awe,
　And thus the mountain chief addressed:
"Now canst thou break the sacred law
　By which your royal sires were blessed,
With war on Achmed and your child,
　Betrothed by Rostam's prudent zeal,
And leagued with rebels rude and wild
　A peaceful monarch's throne assail?"

"Cease, noble Georgian, prythee cease,
To laud a tyrant's love of peace,
Whose realm is crimsoned with a flood
Of innocent and loyal blood;
By whom our faith sublime, adored,
Is persecuted, cursed, abhorred,
And the grand agent we revere,
That beams in beauty from each sphere,

Adorning now the veil of night,
That robes the sun in heaven-born light,
And missioned by the will divine
New orbs to form, new heavens define,
Eternal toils through boundless space,
Our God's illumined dwelling place.
That fire, with which our altars glow, [6]
Is deemed our idol! Fiends, they know
'Tis there, in memory to recall
His kind benevolence o'er all.

" Let Achmed, of descent so true,
    Resign the cause he now defends.
My long lost Mindah, found anew,
    Will then withdraw her Georgian friends:
So shall the tyrant's race be done,
    Just vengeance her due tribute gain,
And Achmed, welcomed as a son,
    In victory o'er Iran reign."

" All powerful passions sense beguile,"
    Said Herman with a languid smile;
" 'Twere easier turn the ocean's stream
    Than Achmed from the paths of fame;
Pledged to uphold in deed and word,
In truth unstained, his sovereign lord.
Nor would a Georgian troop retire
Content, though urged by our desire.
But let thy gallant band recede,
And Maghmud, in his hour of need,

Will shun the war, rebellion cease,
When millions may repose in peace."

"What! from yon city's spoil retire!
　Revenge on the usurper's head!
No! by the altar's sacred fire
　And shades of our immortal dead!
Too long we've suffered by the hand,
　And perjured faith of Abbas' race,
Unhonored in our fatherland—
　The mountain rude our dwelling place.
The hallowed earth whence heaven evolves [7]
　Its awful ministering agent, flame,
Our march to victory dissolves
　From fealty to an impious claim.
Too long the misery of years,
　The agony of hope deferred,
For justice cried, revenge appears,
　Our ardent prayer at length is heard."

"By Christian law for reasons hidden,
Revenge," sighed Herman "is forbidden,
And when presumptuous man essays
His irate madness thus to please;
Misfortune oft to meet him flies,
And make his life the sacrifice.
Improvident you'll lead your host
Of mountain serfs, the rebel's boast,
Mayhap encountering in the strife
　Your daughter's faithful Georgian band,
On her you value more than life,
　Wreaking revenge with blood-stained hand.

"Farewell, unhappy prince, thine oath,
  Pledged on the consecrated fire,
May seal the destiny of both,
  Wrought by an unrelenting sire."

Foreboding sorrow, Herman sought
  The cool breeze of the midnight air,
Leaving the chief oppressed in thought,
  A prey to heart-consuming care.

# THE DOOM OF MAC DIARMID,

## An Oriental Legend of the Gael.

### CANTO VI.

Earth rolled in æther, bared her breast
From the dark pall that robed the west,
Revealing Iran's realm to view,
Bathed in the budding rose's hue.
Soft, dewy smiles her blush adorn;
Responsive to the star of morn,
The glorious sun, whose glances steal,
As though he'd donned a ruby veil,
To mitigate their ardent birth,
In fond solicitude to earth.

Thus lovers, whose affections start
To sudden being, ere the heart
The vital current can retain
From whelming bosom, brow and brain,
While passion doubts—enraptured slave—
Of greater bliss beyond the grave.

Roll on fair orbs through light and shade,
By will divine your paths are made,
Yours is the doom to lovers sweet,[1]
When parted long, again to meet.

Ere brightened into day the dawn,
   Had Achmed the wide camp surveyed,
Where Maghmud's troops, securely drawn,
   In expectation pleased delayed.
Not so, by wasting famine pressed
   Sadly declined the city's crowd;
While Arab warriors slothful rest,
   And treason's muttered low and loud.
Their griefs the aged monarch move
   To lead his faithful followers all,
In arms his country's cause to prove,
   And perish ere his people fall.
Abdallah, eager, pressed his stay
   The mutinous complaints to still;
That he himself would lead the way
   To conquest—such was Allah's will.

Would ye the battle-field behold,
Where knights, arrayed in steel and gold,
Their banners to the breeze unfold,
   In warlike pride elate?
Then see on yonder brilliant plain,
Debouched from Gulnabad a train
Of ordnance, pouring grape like rain,
   Charged with the rebel's fate.

Those columns through the vapour's gloom,
Whose turbaned warriors darkly loom,
Where loud the guns resounding boom,
    The central van compose.
Remote the dusky squadrons seem
Of Arabs on the left extreme;
The right, where flashing sabres gleam,
    The gallant Georgians close.

Fear, to ambition oft allied,
Induced Mir Maghmud late to bide
In tents enclosed with trenches wide,
    By narrow causeways spanned;
There, as from camp his troops recede,
Now lingering, now with flurried speed,
Numbers assailed from batteries bleed
    By Persian foresight planned.
Still as the Afghans, side by side,
With quickening pace, their van supplied,
Their leftward columns scared divide
    O'ercome by panic dread;
For on their front in force advance,
Whose former deeds their dread enhance,
Iberia's horse with sword and lance
    By Achmed nobly led.

Maghmud in vain exclaimed," A prize,
To royal spoil exalt your eyes,
May Monkir doom the knave that flies [2]
    To death in livid flame."

Among the chieftains thus addressed
One with his ardent followers pressed,
When piercing through his guarded breast
   A Georgian weapon came.
Recoiling with instinctive fear,
Mutely they gaze, alarmed to hear
The conqueror's triumphant cheer;
   Mir Maghmud turned dismayed;
When, as his columns wavering swerve,
The Tartar horse, his chos'n reserve,
Advancing with unshaken nerve,
   The onset firmly stayed.

For courage, strength, and stature famed,
Their Hetman, Oman Oglou named,
Chiding, his compatriots blamed,
   Who shunned the Georgian chief.
"On, dastards, on! a guerdon's there,
Of arms that none but princes wear,
A steed well worth a province fair,
   For one encounter brief."
With rapid and augmented force
They plunge, the plain beneath their course
With arms resounds and clang of horse
   Conjoined in deadly strife.
"Beware Mac Diarmid, caution take
To deeds of instant danger wake;
They fight not now for conquest's sake,
   They combat for thy life."

## CANTO VI.

A Georgian lord thus anxious cried,
In warning tone at Achmed's side,
Then pressed his powerful roan to ride
   Against the Tartar's spear.
His lance at Oglou's bosom aimed,
By force diverged, his charger maimed,
The rider gaunt with rage inflamed,
   Unsheathed a falchion sheer,
And in the noble Georgian's crest,
So deep the weighty steel impressed,
He could not thence the weapon wrest,
   Till broke the tempered blade.
Though grieved to death was Achmed's heart,
No moistening sign his eyes impart,
Whence flashing fire appeared to start,
   As one wild bound he made.
His black horse spurred, beneath him flew
More swiftly than the light sea-mew,
Yet Oglou met him armed anew,
   With massive spear and sword.
The ponderous spear was whirled aside
By Achmed's lance, which, opening wide
The Hetman's breast, a purple tide
   The earth profusely gored.
As some tall, tapering round tower, grown [2]
By age more firm, though fiercely blown
Through winter's storms, at length o'erthrown
   By lightning from its base,
Cemented falls, yet still entire,
Though blighted by the scathing fire:

Thus Oglou falls, while frantic ire
   Convulsed his ghastly face.
The tumult swelled the corse around
The Tartars scorning to yield ground
Stung by revenge and grief profound,
   Though numbers slaughtered fell;
The dastard with despairing groan,
The listless with a languid moan,
In silence still—the brave alone
   No sign of suffering tell.

Meantime the cannon's deafning roar
Is heard the central battle o'er,
   Where vapours dense and grey,
Embroidered as with fleece of snow,
Charged with the lurid lightning's glow,
   Obscure the doubtful day.

Where combats now the squadron rare,
So pleased the tide of war to bear,
   By Kerman's chieftain led?
As high in air the vapour floats,
Yon glittering spear-armed band denotes
   Mir Maghmud's bulwark dread.
Arranged in close-formed, hollow square,
Why gaze they still inactive there
   On yon opposing force?
Though well recruited, sure they know
Their late contemned, disheartened foe,
   The light-armed Arab horse.

## CANTO VI.

Yet chafed the gallant mountaineer,
Indignant in the ranks to hear
   No signal of advance;
While frequent the artillery's boom,
That wafts the brave an early doom,
   Clouds his appalling glance.

Prone to assault expectant foes,
'Twas marvelled why the Arab chose
   His matchless steeds to rein.
The loyal, unsuspecting deemed,
A liegeman true it well beseemed
   A threat'ning charge to feign;
While volley after volley flew,
And Afghan crowds and Guebres slew
   With sure and deadly aim.
But treason foul will oft unnerve
The cause the traitor's bribed to serve,
   While branding guilt and shame.
Though now, when frequent peals of fire
Made Maghmud's lessening ranks retire,
   And Fortune on her right
Bade Persia smile; and Tartars fly
Before the Georgian chivalry,
   Defeated in the fight.
Abdallah from the war recedes,
Nor taunting shout, nor uproar heeds
   Retreating from the plain;
Abhorring his accursed designs,
No panic seized the royal lines
   Though fraught with conscious pain.

By renovated ardour led
The Afghans, while the Arab fled,
   Arrest their slow retreat,
Then rush o'er prostrate comrades slain,
So vast their numbers yet remain,
The conquering foe to meet.

The field, with cautious eye surveyed,
To Herman anxious doubt conveyed,
   As on the Afghans came.
The guns, before so happ'ly plied
He now with zeal more freely tried
   In one broad sheet of flame.
Then, as the dying groans he hears,
Ere slow the war-smoke disappears,
   Above the field of blood,
One charge, wherewith the foemen reel,
He made, contending steel with steel,
   While yet dismayed they stood.
Commingled in the tumult dire
With scant resistance they retire,
While star-like beams the sparkling fire
   From falchion blade and lance;
Again the rebel hosts recede,
Their leaders fallen or wounded bleed,
When in their deadliest hour of need
   The Guebre troops advance.

On Herman's left their columns fell,
Who deemed their clashing spears the knell
Of battle lost, whose waves now swell
   Like surges of the deep,

When winds in storm contending blow,
And heave the driven foam like snow,
His turbanned warriors, 'gainst the foe
　　Like billows sink to sleep :
For dearth had stol'n their strength away,
Their sword arms wearied with the fray,
O'ercome with toil since dawning day,
　　Yet still a fervour shone
To light the glittering, closing eye,
Repel the pain, repress the sigh,
And raise the Moslem spirit high
　　To joys eternal won.

Brave Herman ! shall thy fame and life
Be immolated in the strife ?
　　Sage Nestor of the field !
No ! fame for virtue never dies,
Though lost the victory, angels rise
To guard the noble, just, and wise,
　　With Providence to shield.

Now turns the torrent, veers the brunt
Of horrid war in Persia's front,
　　Where late the Afghans fled.
The flying reassemble there
Bereft of arms, which in despair
They cast away, when on the rear
　　Impending mortal dread;
The Georgian horse with blood-stained swords,
From swift pursuit of Tartar hordes,
　　Returned with rapid stride.

Then rose the battle's raging sound,
The agonizing shrieks astound,
The victors shout the dying round,
   And o'er the prostrate ride.

While thus the furious contest stormed,
Ullah perceiving, quick reformed
   His troops in phalanx squared;
And proud within his stalwart lines
To Maghmud and his suite assigns
A safe retreat, whom fear inclines
   Or Georgian weapons spared.

Their pallor, panting, speed evince
Their terrors, as they shout "The prince!"
   For Achmed, still arrayed
In princely arms, his van commands,
Charging Mir Maghmud's scattered bands,
Where'er the rebel horde withstands
   The spear or trenchant blade.

Ullah remarkèd with flashing eyes
Before the Georgian leader rise
   In havoc heaps of slain;
And fierce with wrath on Abbas' line,
Chose of his bravest veterans nine,
Who should by preconcerted sign,
   His deadly course restrain.

From Alpine heights the mountain snow
Succumbing fills the vale below
   With desolation wide;

## CANTO VI.

'Till, when the sun's dissolving fire
Derobes the valley's pure attire,
And timid flocks again respire
   To bask in Summer's tide.
Thus Achmed o'er the field had gone,
Leading his dauntless warriors on,
   Whose waving plumes seemed tost
Like drifted snow unsullied, spread
Above the dying and the dead,
Far as the timid Afghans fled,
   To Kerman's fiery host.

But, as enticed by deathless fame,
And heat of war's inspiring flame,
On Ullah's bristling ranks they came,
   Alas! his faithful band;
As when Burgundia's chieftain bold [4]
His daring chivalry enrolled
Against Helvetia's mountain hold—
   Dear freedom's favoured land—
Fell numerous o'er the prostrate foes
Their weapons doomed to long repose,
While higher still the turmoil rose
   The sanguined plain above;
"Again Mac Diarmid lead," they cry,
"We'll follow thee, on thee rely—
If lost the day, at least we'll die
   Around the chief we love."

Again they charge the threat'ning wood
Of spears in which the Guebres stood;
While torrents on each side of blood
    Announce more deadly toil.
The reckless, the tremendous course,
The impetus of man and horse
O'erwhelm the van of Ullah's force,
    Who, stunned, at length recoil.
Then mingled in confusion wild
Spearman and steed in slaughter piled,
    Round Achmed raged the fight,
Whom Allah's chosen braves assail,
Till broken are their weapons frail,
They turn in stupor, mute and pale,
    To ignominious flight.

Irate, the Sultan Guebre flew
To chide their fears, their arms renew;
Point to their wearied foes, how few
    The combat yet sustained.
He leads them on now less alarmed,
Repels the Georgians, 'till disarmed
By Achmed's hand, and left unharmed,
    Yet hostile wrath remained;
To owe his life, oh! dire disgrace!
To one of that destested race,
    Indignantly he cries,
"Children of Mithra, mountaineers,
Whoe'er yon glorious sun reveres,
Enclose the foe with circling spears,
    The knave who falters, dies."

As Kerman's sons the stern behest
Obeyed in masses densely pressed,
Thrice did Iberian courage test
   Their rude disciplined zeal.
Woe worth the hour! fair Georgia's pride
Fell bleeding by Mac Diarmid's side,
What vails it that a sanguined tide
   The Guebres loss reveal :
For now in denser numbers round
They close ; no pause, no rest is found,
While thundering swelled the battle's sound
   As Ætna's deepening roar ;
Achmed at length beneath the showers
Of darts is whelmed.
          "Eternal powers ! !"
They shout, " the Chelminar is ours ! !
   The prince survives no more."

    \*   \*   \*   \*   \*   \*

Contention dies, as flame recedes
From the wild prairie's flowers and weeds
   In Mississippi's vale ;
For Persia's blighted arms oppose
No more a front to hostile foes ;
While mourning round the fall'n they close—
   Their hope, their pride, their weal.

A dread sensation, still, profound,
Pervades the late contested ground.
   The Georgians, plunged in grief,

All deeply scarred with wounds are seen
To weep the loved one of their queen,
Whom now they raise their arms between,
   Their late devoted chief.

Ullah's stern pride, his vengeance all
Ceased as he saw the hero fall;
   Remorsefully he rushed,
And from the head the turban drew,
By the warm stream 'twas crimsoned through,
   That from the temple gushed.

Then flew with woe-impassioned mien
Kind Herman to the fatal scene;
   From Achmed's breast he tore
The caftan, robe, and princely dress,
Life's effluent current to repress,
   And wandering sense restore.

Then ope'd the languid, dying eye,
Pale as a star in dawning sky,
   To look immoved above;
And dwell on scenes long passed away,
When Mindah's smile, or Diarmid's lay,
Shed rapture o'er life's early day,
   Replete with holy love.
The passing gale a brighter glow
Diffusing o'er his pallid brow
   Received the parting sigh,

That faintly with a smile expressed
The last dear thought that warmed his breast,
'Twas " Dulce et decorum est
   Pro patria mori."


Ere still in death his limbs repose,
The loosened folds of dress disclose
   To Ullah's wondering eyes
A jewelled girdle, mystic, rare,
Which none but Mithra's princes wear.
   With startling awe he cries :
" How should a Moslem of the line
Of Abbas bear yon sacred sign,
Impressed with characters divine ? "
   Herman in scorn replied :
" Stain not the memory of the dead ;
Thy rage has but too deeply sped,
Revolving on thine aged head
   The fruit of vengeance tried ;
For know, though Kerman's tears like rain
May fall, 'tis Diarmid's son you've slain,
   Flower of thy race I ween.
Rostam's adopted heir alone
Blessed her betrothed with yon rich zone,
   Well worthy of a queen.


" In memory of her infant days,
That amulet she loved to praise.
   When life's last hope was o'er.

On yester e'en a faintness came,
She spoke of life's departing flame,
Bequeathed the gem—called Achmed's name ;
  This morn she breathed no more."

A deadly agonizing pain,
Assailing Ullah's heart and brain,
  His sense o'er paralysed.
He cast him on the lifeless clay,
Conjured Mac Diarmid's soul to stay,
And Iran rule with gentle sway,
  But not as Moslem guised.
Invoked his daughter to abide
An earthly crown—her Achmed's bride.
  As smote with frenzy wild,
He reck'd not Hussein came to yield
His throne, the people's lives to shield,
But prostrate on the gory field,
  Raved for his long lost child.

Israfil, soaring in regions of light, [5]
  Wakened the voice of the blissful above,
Mingling in melody charms ever bright,
  Purity radiant, immaculate love.

Wafted in glory, come warrior of earth,
  Free from thy mutable prison of clay.
Heaven, that adorned the land of thy birth,
  Smiles on her children though exiled away.

Long have they toiled in the land of the stranger,
  Roaming unhouselled, unequalled in name ;
Peerless in battle, undaunted in danger,
  Lighting with lustre the annals of fame.

## CANTO VI.

Gifted and honoured, the sons of the lyre
   In sanctity hallowed their own native isle;
When sweeter, more holy, in accents of fire
   Ascended the voice of good Diarmid the while.

On life's troubled ocean, in sorrow serene,
   To freedom and country devoted he gave
A heart whose divine aspiration had been
   To liberty sacred, though helpless to save.

Endeared to the throne of the mystical dove
   Is the child of the faithful, the race of the bard,
Last hope of aged Diarmid, the mansion of love
   Opes bright to receive thee, while angels will guard.

To the smile of thy now sainted Mindah portraying
   Delight never told of thy welcome is given;
In human affliction, no longer arraying
   Those eyes beaming beauty immortal in heaven.

# THE DOOM OF MAC DIARMID,

## An Oriental Legend of the Gael.

### NOTES TO CANTO I.

(1)—*Haste to the court, the Meidan gain.*

The Meidan was an extensive avenue leading to the palace, through which, on all solemn occasions, most gorgeous processions were accustomed to pass. It had on each side rows of splendid trees; and derived its name from the space or quantity of ground it contained, as *meid* in the ancient language of Persia—which was identical with the Irish—signified quantity, and *tan*, land: hence comes the term *atmeidan*, a racecourse or hippodrome; the prefix *at*, or *ata*, serving to designate the term as an open plain.

(2)—*Chilminar.*

This word is probably compounded of *cill*, a spacious edifice or castle, though more usually applied to a church, *min*, fine, and the possessive pronoun *ar*, our, and not as some would have it, of Arabic words signifying forty pillars. See *O'Reilly's Irish Dictionary* for these components, with Dr. O'Donovan's *Supplement*.

## NOTES TO CANTO II.

(1)—*The pepul boughs, the rose's leaves.*

The pepul is a species of poplar—a favourite tree in Persia.

(2)—*Visions appear, as if yon sun*
  *Stored sacred beams to light our fanes.*

It was a law and custom of the ancient Persians, that at certain periods of the year all ordinary fires should be extinguished, and that none should be rekindled unless from the flame consecrated in their temples. The same custom is recorded to have existed in Ireland in the age of Ollam Fodla. At the time of the Summer's solstice, when the sun, or *mithra*, as the Persians conceived, had attained his greatest exaltation; when they believed the creative and beneficent power had triumphed over the power of evil, and they beheld what they deemed the result of the victory—the earth adorned in profusion with fruits and flowers, and all creatures rejoicing in the exuberant gifts of a bounteous providence—at this period their joy was expressed by the exhibition of numerous fires, with which every hill and valley of their beautiful and fertile country was illuminated. This custom has been handed down through successive ages, and is still as invariably practised at the same period of the year in the west of Ireland, as when the early followers of Zoroaster first migrated to the Island of Destiny.

(3)—*From Scotia's isle of hallowed fame.*

Scotia was the name by which Ireland was designated and best known for many centuries. It was said to have been derived from Scota—wife of Milesius—whose descendants settled in the country. There are many, however, incredulous as to this derivation, although it certainly appears as well authenticated as any other historical record of equal antiquity. Moreover it was usual with the inhabitants to give the country the name of some favourite queen, as Fire, Banba, Fodla, etc.

## NOTES TO CANTO III.

(1)—*'Tis not the Afghan you oppose,
Imbued with our unsullied faith.*

The Arabs and Afghans were of the same sect in religion; both, in common with the Turks, holding in veneration Abubeker, Omar, and Othman as the successors of Mahomet. The Persians, on the other hand, considered Ali as the rightful successor, and did not participate with the former in the belief that the Koran was a gift communicated directly from heaven. There are many other differences between the two sects which are, however, of less importance.

(2)—*He should the Sultan Guebre wound.*

Among the Arabs, Sultan Guebre signified king of fire; this title was given by them to Napoleon Buonaparte, after his splendid victory over the Mameluke cavalry in Egypt. The term sultan is of Persian origin—compounded of *sult*, the delight, and *tan*, the land. It was first applied to Mahomed Ghizni, who invaded India, and spoiled it of immense wealth. The word *Guebre* has a like origin from an ancient term signifying fire, and probably compounded of *ga*, a ray, and *bar*, above; whence General Vallancey derives Gabriel, the angel of fire; gaba, a smith or worker in fire, etc. All these components are identical in Irish.

(3)—*That Mithra's progeny were charmed.*

Mithra was the name given by the ancient Persians to the sun, which they allegorically personified and revered as a being next to Ormusd in power and benevolence. They were frequent observers of the celestial luminaries, and to explain their motions had invented artificial cycles and spheres, which were kept by the Magi in caves, called the caves of Mithra. The Magi possessed more knowledge of philosophy, particularly of astronomy, than the rest of mankind; in which, however, they permitted no foreigners to be initiated but such as were distinguished for learning and wisdom; of this number were Pythagoras and Thales.

They were acquainted with the precession of the equinox, and its period; and in the arts of mining, metallurgy, weaving, dyeing, etc. attained a proficiency unknown to Europe for many subsequent ages. According to Mizami they were remarkably celebrated for their skill in music and painting. They delighted to be called children of the sun—*Mac Mithra* —a name identical with Mac Murrogh, so common amongst their descendants, the ancient Irish.

(4)—*The dart was pointed at his breast.*

"The Arabs by constant practise become so expert in throwing the lance, that it is not thought an extraordinary feat to bear off a ring on the point of a javelin."— *Richardson, Dissert.*

(5)—*Their patient camels daily trained*
*To bear huge guns.*

The advantage gained by Mir Maghmud, in his first engagement with the king's forces, was entirely due to this novel expedient of having dromedaries thus trained and accoutred; which, when the Persian cavalry approached, caused such a stampede among the horses, that it was impossible to bring them to the encounter.

(6)— *while the kuzzlebash*
*Oft on their lines resistless dash.*

The kuzzlebash were favorite troops in the Persian army. The term is probably derived from *cusal,* courage, and *bas,* death.—See *O'Reilly's Irish Dictionary.*

## NOTES TO CANTO IV.

(1)—*Shiraz in splendour once outvied.*

Shiraz is compounded of *sior*—perpetual or immortal, and the assertive verb *is.*—See *Irish Dictionary.*

(2)—*The winsome banks of Rocnabad.*

Rocnabad is probably compounded of *rognaithe*, chosen, and *bad*, of love. It was celebrated in one of the lyrics of Hafiz, the Persian poet; thus translated by Sir Wm. Jones:

"Boy, let yon liquid ruby flow,
  And bid thy pensive heart be glad;
Whate'er the frowning zealots say,
  Tell them their Eden cannot shew
A stream so clear as Rocnabad,
A bower so sweet as Mosellay."

Mosellay was an oratory; probably compounded of *mo*, my, and *sleacd*, devotion or prayer.—See *Irish Dictionary.*

(3)—*No treason foul nor impious fraud
     Their sanguinary deeds outlawed.*

As an instance of fidelity to their engagements, it is related by Gibbon, that the Arabs, having subdued Persia, brought Harmozan, the satrap of Susa, a prisoner to their caliph, Omar, with the view of having him immediately executed, as he had given them the greatest resistance. After a painful conference, the Persian complained of thirst, but manifested some apprehension, lest they should kill him while drinking. "Be of good courage," said the caliph, "your life is safe till you have drank this water;" the satrap accepted the assurance, and instantly dashed the vase containing the water to the ground. Omar would have avenged his disappointment, but his companions represented the enormity of a caliph violating his pledge. Harmozan obtained a free pardon, and subsequently, with a view probably to conciliate him, a pension of two thousand pieces of gold.

(4)—*Isfahan deep thy people felt*
        *Treason's abhorred, infernal art.*

It was said of Isfahan, that previous to the irruption of the Afghans it contained 250,000 inhabitants; and that a considerable portion of the commerce of India was, by means of caravans, conveyed to the city, by which it was immensely enriched. At the conclusion of the war its population scarcely amounted to 30,000: so that this rebellion was as destructive to Persia as the invasion of either Zingis or Tamerlane.

## NOTES TO CANTO V.

(1)—*Who dared to combat fire so dread*
     *That from their hallowed shrine was spread.*

The ancient Persians, followers of Zoroaster, considered it a sacrilege to extinguish the consecrated fire, which was kept constantly burning in their temples, no matter how valuable the property that might be consumed by it.— See *Hyde de Religione Persarum.*

(2)—*Who in thine ancient annals versed,*
      *Knows not what glory in the west*
       *Adorned a branch of Mithra's race.*

Upwards of one thousand years previous to the Christian era, a colony called the Tuatha de Danaan—children of song—settled in Ireland. In the arts of civilization they were superior to the generality of the people then existing in Europe, which has been satisfactorily proved by the discovery of various relics—as torques, chains, crowns of gold, etc.—in different parts of the country, all of which are so well known to antiquarians, as indicative of a Persian origin. A circumstance that manifests their early acquaintance with letters is shown by the discovery of their seals, which were of porcelain. About one hundred of these have been found in different parts of Ireland, remote from each other, impressed with figurative or ideographic characters, after the manner of the Chinese; whence they have been called "Chinese porcelain seals," although it is most probable that all nations, from China westward to Mexico, commenced their written communications in the same manner. Phonetic signs, it is generally believed, were a subsequent invention. The experience of this people in the art of mining was not clearly ascertained until about a century ago; when, in a partially-worked coal mine near Ballycastle, in the county Antrim, implements and expedients for mining were discovered similar to those in modern use, but in such a state of rust and decay, as to show they had not been used for many thousand years. The Tordetani, described by Strabo as having colonized part of the Spanish peninsula, were probably of the same race, as might be inferred from their having their laws, annals, and institutions, transmitted in *song* for an indefinite number of generations. They are said to have claimed an antiquity of 6000 years.

(3)—*That skill in harmony divine*
*Revealed to ancient Greece alone.*

While other nations divided the octave into tones and semitones, the bards of Greece went still further—discerning and employing the quarter-tone in their melodies. See *Gillies' History of Greece.*

(4)—*Ullah intent the scroll surveys*
*Suspended in a lambent blaze.*

The zones or girdles which the ancient Persian was in the habit of wearing, were made of various constituents, such as silk, wool, camel or goat's hair, leather, or even of asbestos, the last of which must have been the material in the present instance. They were generally, when worn by the higher ranks, adorned with gold, silver, and precious stones, and dyed with various figures and characters by some chemical preparation, in the invention and composition of which the ancient artists were not inferior to those of the present day.

(5)—*By Ormusd in their natal hour, etc.
Children of Amita, etc.*

In investigating the ancient religion of the Persians, great misapprehension has occurred by considering Ormusd and Amita as two distinct beings, whereas the latter term is merely an attribute of the former. *Ormusd* or *Oirmid*, whom they acknowledged and adored as the creator, signifies worship or adoration. *Amita*, on the other hand, means eternal or everlasting, being compounded of *am*, time, and *ite* or *iteac*, consuming; that is to say, time-consuming.—See *Irish Dictionary*. It is not unusual to substitute the attribute for the being understood, particularly in oriental phraseology. Even in our greatest modern poet we find the very same attribute applied in a like sense:

" Or that the *Everlasting* had not fixed
His canon 'gainst self-slaughter."

The religion of the ancient Persians differed in no essential particulars from that of the Jews, as may be inferred from a careful study of the first chapter of Ezra, where Cyrus is represented in the beginning of his reign, as using all the available means of his empire to rebuild the temple of Solomon, and restore the sacred vessels of gold and their appurtenances, used in the administration of the divine service. The conquest of Cyrus, however, over the idolatrous kings of Assyria and Babylon, was remarkable, not only for the restoration of the Jews and their temple, but also for the restoration of an empire that existed for many centuries previous to the reign of kings in Nineveh and Assyria. Sir William Jones, whose investigations in oriental history were conducted with such zealous and indefatigable research, was the first to direct attention to this once populous and flourishing empire. According to his description, it extended from the Caucasian mountains to the Himalayas, the river Sind or Indus extended its boundary in the latter direction, while the sea of Oman constituted one of its southern limits; so that it must have comprised the present territories of Persia, Georgia, Afghanistan, Turkestan, etc., together with Asia Minor. When, however, it was torn asunder by contention, chiefly arising from religious dissentions, a considerable number of the inhabitants emigrated to the surrounding countries. The fanaticism of the first body of exiles who colonized India was so intense, that they enacted a law prohibiting their return.

From the remains of an old work called the Dabistan, which treated of twelve different religious sects, and was said to have been compiled by an ancient Cashmerian named Mobsan Fani, Sir William Jones was enabled, by the aid of a learned Brahmin, to derive the few particulars disclosed to us relative to this, the oldest monarchy on earth; its flourishing condition under many generations of kings, particularly that of the Mahabadian dynasty; its partition into Iran and Turan, and the various and complicated divisions that occurred, when idolatry, similar to that which degraded the Israelites after the reign of Solomon, exerted its baneful influence in opposition to the monotheistic faith. The chief apostle of this faith in the primeval empire was Zerdusht or Zoroaster, represented by Greek historians as having lived some thousand years before the reign of Darius Hystaspes. He, it was said, compiled the ancient Zendavesta, which was lost when the Arabs overran Persia, destroyed Ctesiphon, and burned its celebrated libraries.

The followers of Zoroaster had adopted customs and institutions so like those of the Jews, as to create a difficulty in distinguishing any important difference between them. The magi or priests of the former, similar to the tribe of Levi, were supported by tithes of all the produce of the country; they it was that at the nativity, **guided** by a **star from** heaven, **came to** Bethlehem, bearing gold, frankincense and myrrh, **to hail with joy** the advent of the Redeemer; and, inspired by a Divine visitation, avoided the communication of their knowledge to Herod. In the tabernacles of both a constant fire was kept, replenished by the tribe of Levi with oil in golden lamps, morning and evening, and with incense on a golden altar, which was conveyed along with them during their wanderings in the desert.

**The Magi,** with **the most precious** woods renewed their fire, and bearing it **on a silver** tripod, accompanied Darius on all his expeditions. What but the most unlimited hope and confidence **in the God** of Israel, as the guardian of the **innocent, would have forced** Darius **to submit Daniel to the fury of wild beasts**—in compliance with an imperative **law—while he fasted and prayed** for his preservation? The unavoidable inference issuing from these and other considerations, **too** numerous to detail, moreover, that it was occasionally called the religion of Abraham by D'Herbelot, Hyde, and other candid authorities, compel us to believe that the religion of the ancient Persians was a pure monotheism, and that its devotees, when impotent to subdue the host of idolaters that rebelled against them, abandoned their native land in considerable numbers, in search of a more desirable abode. It was probably the contest, thus terminating, that laid the foundation of the Greek fable of the war between the Titans and the Gods; the deities, as understood by its author, being the objects of the Sabian or other idolatrous worship; the Titans, on the other hand, adhering to the **pure and** original faith, their name being synonymous with MacMithra, or children of the sun.

However this may be, there can be no doubt that an enlightened and devotedly religious Persian colony settled in Ireland at this remote period; whence the antients named the country the Sacred Island; **as Festus** Aviensus asserts,

> Ast hinc duobus in *Sacram* sic Insulam,
> Dixere *prisci*, etc, etc. . . .
> . . . late genus Hibernorum colit.

Thus we have evidence of the sanctity that even the heathen assigned to the land, ages before the advent of Christianity; and on that glorious and eventful occasion, we find the Magi of Ireland, instead of opposing the doctrine preached by St. Patrick, embracing it with joy, and becoming the ordained Christian ministers, as of an expected revelation.—See Notes in *Reeves' Adamnan*.

To those versed in the Irish vernacular, the proper names in the preceding note will be significant, as it is well known that all such terms were generally compounded of epithets expressive of the attributes of the object indicated: thus, Mahabad is composed of *bad*, love or favour, with the possessive pronoun prefixed; as to the boundaries of the empire under the dynasty which he founded, Caucasian is probably named from *cad*, high, and *cosaint* a defence; Himalaya, from *imiol*, a boundary; Sind, the Indus, from *sin*, to extend; and the sea of Oman, its southern limit, was so called from *oman*, which signifies fear, froth, terror, a name peculiarly assignable to it by those as yet strangers to the art of navigation, except perhaps in the tideless waters of the Mediterranean. The original empire having been divided, the northern portion was styled Turan from *tuaig* the north, while *Iran* retained its name, derived from *iar* the west. The nomenclature of the different provinces of Persia is equally remarkable, *e.g.*, Laristan, which means the middle province, is compounded of *lar*, the middle, the assertive verb *is*, and *tan*, land; Farsistan, of *fars-aing*, wide or ample—the latter syllable of the adjective being omitted in composition, for the sake of brevity—*is* and *tan* as in the preceding appellation; Chorasan of *caora*, grapes, and Erivan of *carrai*, the spring season of the year; the word *tan*, as a component in the two latter provincial names, losing the *t* for the sake of euphony, a practise almost invariably observed in the language.

On the road eastward from Babylon, near the western borders of Media, there is observable a remarkable eminence, terminating a range of hills seventeen hundred feet high, which was considered sacred. It is called Behistan, *i.e.*, the land of wild beasts, from *beist* and *tan*, probably in consequence of its being exempt from other inhabitants. In the surface of this hill, imbedded in the rock with molten lead, are polished stones, at about five hundred feet from its base, on which are inscriptions in the cuneiform character, which were clearly elucidated by Sir Henry Rawlinson, the eminent antiquarian and Sanscrit scholar, whose investigations have thrown such light on the disinterred ruins of Assyria, Phœnicia, and Chaldea. The following are extracts from the inscriptions at Behistan:—
"I am Darius, the great king, the king of kings. The king, my father, was Hystaspes, of Hystaspes the father was Arsames, of Arsames the father was Arigmanes, of Arigmanes the father was Teispes, of Teispes the father was Achæmenes; on that account we have been called Achæmenians. From antiquity we have been unsubdued; from antiquity our race have been kings. By the grace of Ormusd I have become king; Ormusd has given me the empire."

The names in the foregoing inscription may have been derived from terms common to the ancient Persian and Irish dialects. Thus Hystaspes may have been deduced from *is tasc*, expressive of fame or renown; Arsames, from *arsac*, old; Arigmanes, from *arig*, chief; Teispes, from *teisd*, esteem; Achæmenes, from *acmuin*, wealth or power; and Darius, from *darrioga*, a superior to kings. There is reason to believe that it was in the reign of the last-mentioned sovereign, on the occasion of the deliverance of Daniel from his dreadful ordeal, that the Persian judges enacted the celebrated decree, "τω βασιλευοντι Περσεων εξειναι ποιειν το αν βουληται.

Chosroes, the name by which Cyrus is known in Eastern languages, is compounded of *cos*, the foot, with *ro* and *is*, signs of the superlative degree, which taken together signify "most excellent on foot." The Titans were so called from *Titan* the sun.

To these may be added the names of other distinguished rulers, whose memory is still revered by the Parsees; as Cayomers, from *caom*, kind; Husang, from *usa*, just, and *ang*, great; and Afrasiab, from *an*, the, *fras*, liberal, and *ab*, father. "The spider has wove his web in the imperial palace; and the owl hath sung her watch-song in the towers of Afrasiab."

>(6)—*That fire with which our altars glow*
>    *Is deemed our idol!*

It is well known that the ancient Persians were accused as idolators and worshippers of fire by their invaders and persecutors. Firdausi, the poet, however, though himself a Moslem, in describing the worship of Cyrus and his paternal grandfather, for an entire week before the fire on the altar, alludes to them more candidly in nearly the following terms.

>Oh! think not they the fire adored,
>    Whose beam illumed their tearful eyes.
>To Ormusd—God supreme and Lord—
>    Alone they poured repentant sighs.
>
>Seven days before his blazing shrine,
>    Whose flame for ever Heavenward tends,
>To him they prayed—the source divine—
>    On whom eternal life depends.

>(7)—*The hallowed earth, whence Heaven evolves,*
>    *Its awful ministering agent, flame,*

On the southern shores of the Caspian Sea, petroleum or naphtha has been found in beds, so near the surface that the inhabitants make use of them for lighting their habitations, by thrusting reeds or tubes into the earth, through which the vapour passing from beneath, and, being lighted

8

above, affords a very convenient gas-light. They also use them for their culinary preparations. Situate in the vicinity of these bituminous beds, recent travellers have discovered foundations and ruins of magnificent edifices, which, no doubt, at a former very remote period, constituted temples of worship for the disciples of Zoroaster. Similar beds are to be found near Baku, on the western shore, at an inconsiderable distance from the Caspian gates of the Caucasus.

## NOTES TO CANTO VI.

(1)—*Yours is the doom to lovers sweet*
  *When parted long again to meet.*

In a *brochure* published in the year 1858, I suggested that the earth and other planets formerly must have constituted a portion of the sun, and consisted of the same matter sublimated, attenuated, and evolved into the immense surrounding space by the extreme intensity of heat; and subsequently, after an indefinite period, losing their extreme temperature, were condensed into globes according to a universal law to which all matter is subject.

The theory therein described has been since in a great measure corroborated by the discovery of Kirchof and Bunsen of the spectral analysis, and the observations made thereby on the sun, particularly during its eclipse.

The laws of attraction compel us to believe that they are eventually destined to return to their centre of gravitation.

(2)—*May Monkir doom the knave that flies*
  *To death, etc.*

Monkir and Nakir were the angels of death according to Moslem mythology, and Eblis the name of the arch-fiend himself.

The ancient Persian and Irish name for Satan was Ahriman—compounded of *ar*, slaughter or destruction, and *mana*, the cause.

(3)—*As some tall* **tapering round tower,** *grown*
　　By age more firm, *etc.*

An indisputable proof of the descent of the Irish from the ancient followers of Zoroaster, may be deduced from the round towers, so numerous in many parts of Ireland.

Although these edifices were, a long time subsequent to their erection, used for belfreys, watch-towers, etc., yet that they were originally designed for such purposes is totally indefensible. These towers were in fact called *Torregain*—which signifies kindling towers—from *tor*, a tower, and *again*, to kindle.

It has been observed that at a certain period of the year all fires for domestic purposes were required to be extinguished, and none to be rekindled except from the consecrated flame, kept alive by the watchful care of the Magi. These fires were kept burning in some of the towers after the advent of Christianity. It is even recorded that in Kildare, there was one of them in which the fire was not extinguished until near the close of the twelfth century. The preservation of the consecrated fire, however, was not the sole purpose for which those towers were designed : the Magi considered that the bodies of the dead should be resolved into their primitive elements, before they were consigned to the earth, and consequently had them exposed on the summits of the towers until they were completely desiccated and reduced to a cineritious mass, either by the sun's (Mithra's) heat or by the sacred fire kindled from his beams. The embers of the dead were, after their total or partial incremation, deposited in the earth within the area of the tower.

Now it is evident that if in these edifices the entrance were to have been made on a level with the ground on which they were constructed, the remains of the dead, accumulating within, would after some time impede all ingress to these buildings. To obviate this impediment, the entrance was invariably made at a considerable height from the base, so as to require the use of a ladder to gain admission to them. At Ram Island in Lough Neagh, at Timahoe, and many other places, where these round towers are at present situate, human bones, more or less incinerated, have been found interred within them, together with urns, not inelegantly ornamented, which no doubt formerly contained the ashes of the dead.

The custom of exposing the bodies of the dead on lofty towers was continued to a much later period under the Persian government; for in the sixth century, during the long-continued contest between Chosroes Nushirvan and the emperor Justinian, we find that the Colchians, under their king Gubazes, deserted the former, their prejudices revolting against the law of having the dead bodies of their parents exposed—as they asserted—to the crows and vultures of the air.

The round towers of Persia were mostly destroyed by the Arabs, who considered them as edifices devoted to the idolatrous worship of fire, and being chiefly constructed of *adobes*—bricks burnt in the sun—they were easily dilapidated. In the reign of Nadir Kouli Khan, however, a commercial gentleman named Hanway counted four of them which he observed in his travels. A recent traveller also describes "two circular stone towers of moderate size and height, with conical roofs, admirably constructed, evidently of quite ancient origin, situate on the open space east of the city of Erzeroum." The inhabitants of the vicinity knew not their use; but from the description we cannot be at a loss to conjecture for what purpose they were originally designed.

*(4)—As when Burgundia's chieftain bold*
*His daring chivalry enrolled.*

Charles the bold, Duke of Burgundy, led his army, the finest at that time in Europe, to subjugate the Swiss peasantry, but was defeated at the battle of Nancy. The disappointment so **preyed on** his mind that he became deranged and died **soon after.**

(5).—*Israfil soaring in regions of light.*

Israfil, **the angel of music,** is compounded of *file*, minstrel, with the signs of the emphatic superlative prefixed; signifying thereby the **supreme or most** exquisite minstrel.— See *Irish Dictionary.*

www.ingramcontent.com/pod-product-compliance
Lightning Source LLC
Chambersburg PA
CBHW020126170426
43199CB00009B/660